MW01058320

The right of the people to be secure in their persons, houses, papers and effects, against unreasonable searches and seizures, shall not be violated, and no warrants shall issue, but upon probable cause, supported by oath or affirmation, and particularly describing the place to be searched, and the persons or things to be seized.

U.S. Constitution, Amendment IV

Watergate Prosecutor

William H. Merrill

Michigan State University Press • *East Lansing*

☉ The paper used in this publication meets the minimum requirements of ANSI/NISO
Z39.48-1992 (R 1997) (Permanence of Paper).

 Michigan State University Press
East Lansing, Michigan 48823-5245

Printed and bound in the United States of America.

17 16 15 14 13 12 11 10 09 08   1 2 3 4 5 6 7 8 9 10

LIBRARY OF CONGRESS CATALOGING-IN-PUBLICATION DATA
Merrill, William H.
Watergate prosecutor / William H. Merrill.
p. cm.
Includes index.
ISBN 978-0-87013-805-8 (cloth : alk. paper)
1. Merrill, William H. 2. Special prosecutors—United States—Biography. 3. Watergate
Affair, 1972–1974. 4. Nixon, Richard M. (Richard Milhous), 1913–1994—Impeachment.
5. Political corruption—United States. 6. Political ethics—United States. 7. United States—
Politics and government—1969–1974. I. Title.
KF374.W38M47 2007
345.73'01—dc22
[B]
2007036046

Cover design by Erin Kirk New
Book design by Sharp Des!gns, Inc., Lansing, Michigan

Cover image is of Richard Nixon as he boarded a helicopter for Andrews Air Force Base
after resigning the Presidency August 9, 1974. Photo courtesy of AP Images.

green
press
INITIATIVE   Michigan State University Press is a member of the Green Press Initiative
and is committed to developing and encouraging ecologically responsible
publishing practices. For more information about the Green Press Initiative and the use of
recycled paper in book publishing, please visit www.greenpressinitiative.org.

Visit Michigan State University Press on the World Wide Web at www.msupress.msu.edu

Dedication

The author dedicates these memoirs to his daughters Marisa and Vanessa and their mother Carol, and also to Rick and Ann.

Acknowledgments

The author would also like to recognize and thank Archibald Cox (1912–2004), who was United States Solicitor General under President John F. Kennedy and was the Special Prosecutor for the Watergate scandal. On October 20, 1973, in what became known as the "Saturday Night Massacre," President Nixon ordered that Mr. Cox be dismissed. This infuriated Congress, and numerous bills of impeachment followed shortly. In 1978, the Independent Counsel Act was passed as a direct result of the Saturday Night Massacre.

CONTENTS

FOREWORD

Charles R. Breyer

United States District Judge and Assistant Special Prosecutor,

Watergate Special Prosecution Force, 1973–74

The issue here is how far can the Government go in placing security above freedom. It involves a fundamental paradox since the only hope for security lies in the preservation of freedom. Therefore security can not be defined and enforced at the discretion of one man or a small group of men immune from the restraints of law.

—from the trial notes of William H. Merrill

R ecently, our government confirmed news reports that as part of its "war on terror," it had embarked upon warrantless surveillance of telephone and e-mail communications of United States citizens. While admitting that they were eavesdropping on domestic conversations without a search warrant, various officials, including the President and the Attorney General, defended this program as "reasonable," "very specific," and "targeted at people who had known links to al-Qaeda and related terrorist organizations." Thus, not more than forty years after Watergate, the executive branch was conducting searches of citizens' private communications without customary judicial authorization. That fact, while certainly surprising to those of us who prosecuted the White House Plumbers for conducting a burglary of a citizen's private files to find information for use in a criminal prosecution, was not nearly as disturbing as the public's "ho-hum" reaction to this disclosure. Indeed, media polls disclosed that many Americans felt that such an eavesdropping program, even if unconstitutional, was not offensive. Many say they do not mind if their conversations were overheard, for they have "nothing to hide."

There is a danger in thinking that having nothing to hide means having nothing to protect. As long as the public views constitutional rights solely as a shield for the guilty, the dangers of terrorism will always outweigh the enforcement of these rights. What is missing in the public's calculus is the cost to liberty of ignoring the safeguards contained in the Bill of Rights. These rights protect our way of life—a life in which we allow free discourse, diversity of opinion, due process of law, and, if we choose, privacy of our views.

When I joined Bill Merrill's Plumbers task force in 1973, my employer at the time, the San Francisco district attorney, counseled against my departure. He believed that Watergate was simply politics. To me, the investigation into the break-in of Daniel Ellsberg's psychiatrist's office was about whether persons who hold unpopular views and are charged with criminal conduct were treated fairly by the government. No one on our task force questioned the right of the government to protect secrets; we did, however, question whether the means employed by the government to further national-security concerns were constitutionally appropriate. As we know, security of the country has been the concern of every administration since George Washington. Indeed, Special Prosecutor Archibald Cox was told in no uncertain terms that the Plumbers' prosecution would endanger our security interests. But as we also know, the prosecution of the President's closest advisors did go forward, convictions were obtained, and the nation has survived.

The most remarkable lesson of Watergate is how well our Constitution functions when tested. As the investigation proceeded in 1973 and the first six months of 1974, there was a constant drumbeat of criticism that the Special Prosecutor's inquiry was threatening the ability of the President and the executive branch to govern. It was said that this group of thirty-five upstart lawyers was paralyzing a president and diminishing his power, all to the detriment of our national interest.

Hindsight, however, demonstrates that our legal institutions, as envisioned by the framers of our Constitution, "worked" just fine. Consider just a few of its successes: A free press allowed investigative journalists, with the help of confidential sources, to discover and disclose the many covert operations—burglaries, punitive audits of tax returns of political "enemies," laundered campaign contributions, wiretapping of "unfriendly journalists," and, of course, paying hush money to political operatives in an attempt to obstruct justice. An independent federal judiciary saw a cover-up in process and ordered the Justice Department to conduct a grand jury investigation; a Senate committee, through the use of its subpoena power, discovered tape recordings that provided irrefutable evidence of wrongdoing in the Oval Office; a special prosecutor called for the disclosure of such evidence and, upon being fired by the executive branch for not abandoning this quest, energized public opinion to oppose the termination of the inquiry; the Supreme Court unanimously held that no one is above the law, and that even the chief executive must produce evidence; and finally, a House committee voted on articles of impeachment—all of which ultimately led to the President's resignation. Each one of these steps involved treasured constitutionally protected rights—a free press, an independent judiciary, congressional oversight, and the public's right to seek redress of grievances. Thus, even in a crisis that may have affected the executive's ability to govern, the resolution of this crisis was found in the enforcement of these constitutionally created rights and institutions, not in their circumvention.

Today we hear a similar criticism of our constitutional rights. In a war against terror, we are asked whether we can afford such niceties as the First (press), Fourth (searches by warrant), Fifth (due process of law), Sixth (speedy and public trials, right to counsel), and Eighth (no cruel punishment) Amendments provide. I suggest that two questions be posed before curtailing these rights—first, how convincing is the evidence that the exercise of any of these rights would seriously jeopardize our freedom and safety; and second, whether we want to live in a society that does not have these specific liberties. Bill Merrill's account of this historic inquiry into governmental conduct reminds us that we should be less concerned about what we have to hide than what we have to protect.

PROLOGUE

Pat Shellenbarger

Staff Writer, *The Grand Rapids Press*

"There is no week nor day nor hour when tyranny may not enter upon this country, if the people lose their supreme confidence in themselves—and lose their roughness and spirit of defiance—Tyranny may always enter—there is no charm, no bar against it—the only bar against it is a large resolute breed of men."

—*Walt Whitman, as quoted from the trial notes of William H. Merrill*

William Merrill's possessions are few these days: a bed, a dresser, a 13-inch television, and a bust of his late friend Robert F. Kennedy. His section of the room is separated by a curtain from his roommates: three men who, like him, are broke and veterans of past wars, but otherwise have little in common with him. This place, the Grand Rapids Home for Veterans, has been his address for more than a dozen years, since a stroke left him partially paralyzed and robbed him of his voice, his livelihood, and his marriage. His dignity remains intact.

From the basket of his adult-sized tricycle parked in the hall outside his door, he produced a typed manuscript and offered it with his left hand. The right hung at his side. He smiled the crooked smile that has become his trademark since the stroke and uttered, "God damn." He meant no disrespect. Those words and "Oh, God" are all he can manage and have become his all-purpose expressions of greeting, teasing, sorrow, and in this case, joy that someone finally is interested in the story about his role at a critical moment in American history.

In another time and place, Bill Merrill, now 83, was at the center of a political maelstrom, helping unravel one of the most troubling scandals in American history, an episode known as Watergate. He stared down some of the most ruthlessly powerful men in America—Richard Nixon's crewcut men of steel: John Ehrlichman, Charles Colson, and G. Gordon Liddy, among others—and he put them away.

It was not the first time Merrill had faced tough men. As chief assistant United States attorney in Detroit, he prosecuted mobsters and other assorted thugs. He grew up in Birmingham, an upper-class suburb north of Detroit, enlisted in the U.S. Army Air Force during World War II, graduated from Dartmouth College after the war, then earned his law degree at Yale. He worked for a couple of law firms before joining the U.S. Attorney's Office in the early 1960s. It was in that job that he became close to Robert Kennedy, then attorney general of the United States. When Merrill ran unsuccessfully for Congress as a Democrat in a heavily Republican district near Detroit, Kennedy campaigned for him. When Kennedy ran for president in 1968, Merrill returned the favor, heading his Michigan campaign. After Kennedy was assassinated, Nixon defeated Hubert Humphrey for president in one of the closest elections in U.S. history.

For all his strengths, Nixon was a paranoid man, determined to hold onto power whatever the cost. He surrounded himself with like-minded men more loyal to their president than to the law and willing to commit "dirty tricks" to discredit his enemies. In the summer of 1970, Nixon approved a plan greatly expanding the authority of the FBI and CIA to gather domestic intelligence, then later rescinded it. In June 1971, when the *New York Times,* and later the *Washington Post,* began publishing the Pentagon Papers, the Defense Department's top-secret study of the Vietnam War, Nixon was livid. He tried to stop the publication, but the U.S. Supreme Court ruled against him on First Amendment grounds. Nixon was obsessed with plugging the leaks. Thus was formed a secret team inside the White House known as the Plumbers Unit.

Early the morning of June 17, 1972, five men were arrested inside the Democratic National Committee offices in the Watergate hotel and office complex, apparently intending to fix bugs they had planted earlier. Nixon's press secretary, Ron Ziegler, described the break-in as a "third-rate burglary," but inexorably, the threads of Watergate began leading back to the White House. Nixon and his men fought to cover up the scandal, but there was no stopping the revelations, each pointing piece by piece toward the President.

In May 1973, the United States Senate Watergate Committee began holding nationally televised hearings, and Attorney General Elliot Richardson appointed former solicitor general Archibald Cox as the Special Watergate Prosecutor. In his office at a Detroit law firm, Bill Merrill read about the unfolding scandal and was fascinated. He decided to apply for a job with the Special Prosecutor. It would mean a huge cut in pay, but "what was involved was too important to be measured in those terms," Merrill would write later. "I was intrigued by the thought of becoming a member of the staff. It seemed to be a once-in-a-lifetime opportunity for public service that would involve vital issues of national significance." Cox hired Merrill as associate Watergate special prosecutor and put him in charge of a team investigating the White House Plumbers.

In the years since then, "Watergate" has become the term for the web of scandals that eventually forced Nixon to resign, and a synonym for political corruption. Often forgotten in the three-and-a-half decades since then is that Watergate involved more than the Watergate break-in. After the leak of the Pentagon Papers, Nixon became obsessed with discrediting Daniel Ellsberg, a former defense analyst charged with unauthorized possession of the secret study. Over the Labor Day weekend in 1971, at the instigation of the White House Plumbers, former CIA agent Howard Hunt and former FBI agent G. Gordon Liddy engineered the break-in at the Beverly Hills office of Ellsberg's psychiatrist, searching for any derogatory information about Ellsberg. That burglary became the focus of Merrill's investigation and prosecution, and eventually a key to unraveling the entire Watergate scandal.

"When you look back to Watergate, probably as important as anything that happened was going after the Plumbers Unit," said Daniel Schorr, who covered Watergate for CBS News. "Watergate started and ended with the Plumbers Unit. The prosecution having to do with the Plumbers Unit really is what Watergate was all about." Merrill's assistant Charles Breyer, now a U.S. district judge in San Francisco, believes the guilty verdicts in the Ellsberg case were a key to the later convictions in the Watergate burglary. "There were a number of people who were still of the mind this was a prosecution out to get Nixon," said Breyer, the brother of Supreme Court Justice Stephen Breyer, but Merrill "was quite professional and not doctrinaire. He was very well prepared."

Slowly, methodically, he built his case, hauling the President's men before a grand jury, then facing them in court. He took no joy in it. "Instead, there was a sense of regret about what we had to do," he wrote. "We were forcing some of the most powerful men in the government to appear before us to answer difficult and often embarrassing questions and to explain their answers to our satisfaction." Washington attorney Richard Ben-Veniste, who was on the Watergate Special Prosecutor's staff and more recently the 9/11 Commission, described Merrill as a "type-A personality," yet "very low-key. He had a very distinct Midwest style. He was very highly regarded and did a superb job."

As the special prosecutors closed in, Nixon fired Cox on October 20, 1973—an act that became known as the Saturday Night Massacre. Some members of Cox's staff considered resigning in protest, but Merrill disagreed. "I remember saying that we were up against a tough son-of-a-bitch and that if we were going to be successful, we would have to be just as tough," he wrote. He and the other assistant special prosecutors hunkered down and pressed on. To this day, Merrill believes Nixon intended to disband the Special Prosecutor's Office, but the public outcry was so loud, he could not. Leon Jaworski was appointed to replace Cox, and the investigation resumed.

Years later, after Nixon resigned and was replaced by Gerald Ford, after many of the President's men were in prison, Jaworski recalled the key role Merrill played in dismantling the Watergate scandal. "Merrill built his case as solidly and as painstakingly as a beaver builds a dam," he wrote in his book *The Right and the Power*. "The already threadbare cloak of 'national security' was in tatters by the time he completed his arguments." By then, Merrill had written his own book about the case and called it *Watergate Prosecutor: To Protect and Defend the Constitution*, unpublished until now. For Merrill, that year was the most memorable of his life. For America, it was one of the most trying periods in its history.

The first thing we do, let's kill all the lawyers.

—*Dick the butcher, in William Shakespeare's*

Henry VI, Part 2, 4.2.76–77

Watergate Prosecutor

1

Beginning of the End for Nixon

A society in which faceless men carry out orders that no one
admits the responsibility for giving.

—*from the trial notes of William H. Merrill*

I n the spring of 1973, things began coming apart at the seams for Richard
Nixon. It was a time of confusion for many Americans who had given
Nixon an apparently overwhelming mandate the preceding November.
After only a few weeks into his new term as president, it must have seemed
particularly ironic to Nixon, since his reelection appeared to have vindicated
his statements that McGovern's claims about Watergate were politically
motivated and without substance.

The unraveling began in March when James McCord, one of the defendants convicted of the Watergate burglary in June 1972, wrote Judge Sirica
that perjury had been committed during the trial, and that the defendants
had been pressured to remain silent to protect others.

In April, Patrick Grey resigned as acting director of the FBI in the face of newspaper reports that he had destroyed documents relating to the Watergate break-in.

Like the unfolding of a Greek tragedy, the public learned that two of the Watergate burglars had been involved in a break-in at the office of Daniel Ellsberg's psychiatrist in Los Angeles in September 1971. This revelation occurred near the end of Ellsberg's trial involving charges of having unauthorized possession of classified documents. The break-in at Ellsberg's psychiatrist and certain other actions by the government caused the judge in charge of the trial to conclude that Ellsberg had been denied a fair trial, and the charges against him were dismissed.

Then on April 30, H. R. Haldeman and John D. Ehrlichman, the President's top advisers, resigned, and John Dean, the President's legal counsel, was fired.

2

Appointment as Associate Watergate Special Prosecutor

> What we are involved with is an effort to ensure honest government—a respect for government—the sanctity of the Constitution.
>
> —*from the trial notes of William H. Merrill*

During the early part of May, 1973, Congress and the press began to discuss the appointment of a special prosecutor. I was intrigued by the thought of becoming a member of the staff; it seemed to be a once-in-a-lifetime opportunity for public service that would involve vital issues of national significance. I recognized that there also might be personal and professional advantages.

When it appeared that Archibald Cox would be appointed Special Prosecutor, I contacted Jack Miller, an old friend in Washington who had been assistant attorney general in charge of the Criminal Division of the Department of Justice in the early 1950s when I had been chief assistant United States attorney in Detroit. I asked him to recommend me to Cox. A few days later, Jack phoned and said he had talked to Cox about me. He suggested that I write if I was still interested. That same day, I sent a letter to Cox confirming my interest in becoming a member of his staff.

While I waited, I wondered if I would be making a mistake in leaving the security and certainty of the law firm of which I was a partner in return for the financial and other sacrifices that would have to be made, and the uncertainty of the outcome if I went to work for Cox. The picture of a determined president on the cover of the June 4 issue of *Time,* with the caption "Nixon Fights Back," added to the already troublesome feelings about what I was contemplating. But the more I thought about it, the more convinced I became that the advantages outweighed the risks.

After a few days, I phoned Cox's office to follow up on my letter. I was assured that my inquiry was being considered, and that I would hear something in due course. However, I got the impression that the office was besieged by many applicants, and that the few who were there were too overburdened in attempting to keep up with daily developments to spend much time considering staffing. I learned later that over 1,040 applications had been received. So I invented a trip to Washington on "other business" in order to discuss my application in person.

When I informed my law partners of my decision, one of them responded that he would make more money the next year than I would. I was surprised by such a comment; what was involved was too important to be measured in those terms.

On Tuesday, June 12, I met briefly with James Vorenberg and Philip Heymann, professors from Harvard Law School who had come with Cox to help him staff the office and begin the laborious investigations that followed. We talked about the activities I might become involved in, but at that time, the structure of the staff was vague and indefinite. Whatever developed, my law partner was right: my salary would be less than half of what I was earning in private practice.

Then I met Cox. The meeting was brief and rather strange in view of its purpose. Archie did not question me about my background as an assistant United States attorney, or my views on the role of a prosecutor. Rather, we discussed the importance of the principles that seemed to be at stake, particularly the concept that in our society no one is above the law. I was impressed when Archie mentioned the humbling nature of his job. He went on to say that in reading the grand jury testimony of various individuals in positions of importance and authority whom he had known and admired, he wondered what he might have done under similar circumstances. He said, "I know I would not have done anything which I knew or felt was questionable, but I wonder how I would have reacted if I had known others were involved in such conduct."

On my return to Detroit, the cab driver who was taking me to the airport said he was fed up with the Ervin Committee hearings. The committee had been in session since May 17. I was disappointed in this remark. The Special Prosecutor would need much greater public understanding and support if he were to be successful.

The next day, Vorenberg called and said Cox wanted me to join the staff, and told me they had requested an FBI clearance of me by June 10. Although the clearance had not been completed, Vorenberg phoned on June 18 and asked if I could start right away, subject to the results of the FBI investigation. I agreed to start the next Monday. My eagerness to join the Special Prosecutor's staff was to some extent influenced by the thoughts expressed in a *New York Times* editorial on June 17 entitled "Subverting America," which stated:

> The Watergate scandal is a profoundly sinister event because, in so many of its aspects it reflects an authoritarian turn of mind and a ready willingness on the part of those at the highest levels of government to subvert democratic values and practices. Tyranny was not yet a fact, but the drift toward tyranny, toward curtailing and impairing essential freedoms, was well underway until the Watergate scandal alerted the nation to the danger.
>
> Watergate was a series of crimes and conspiracies against individual liberty, against the democratic electoral process, and against lawful government. Only when the great majority of citizens know the full story of these crimes and conspiracies can the restorative work of reform and renewal begin.

This educational process would be one of the major responsibilities of the Watergate Special Prosecution Force.

My arrival at the office, 1425 K Street, on June 19 was delayed by a monumental traffic jam. The police had blockaded several streets due to a visit by Soviet Premier Brezhnev. Much of that first day was occupied with filling out the inevitable and sometimes incomprehensible government forms and having my picture taken for special identification papers. The indoctrination was completed when I took the oath of office as an associate Watergate special prosecutor, in which I promised "to protect and defend the Constitution of the United States of America."

3

Determining My Role

"God grants liberty only to those who love it, and are always
ready to guard it and defend it."

—*Daniel Webster, 1834, as quoted from the*
trial notes of William H. Merrill

For the first few days, I attempted to assimilate all the material on the
Watergate break-in and the suspected cover-up. There were volumes
of grand jury testimony, congressional committee testimony, FBI
interviews, statements from witnesses, and documentary evidence—much
of which was incomplete or contradictory. I was trying to understand the
lengthy and detailed chronology of events, evaluate the evidence, and determine who might be witnesses and who might be defendants. By the end of
the first week, I had read enough to recognize that we would be confronted
with the argument that the actions we were challenging were justified on
grounds of national security. I wrote a memo to Cox that suggested we
begin the necessary factual and legal research to develop an appropriate
response to such a defense.

There was a sense of urgency in what we were doing because of the public interest in its outcome. As a consequence, we worked long hours, often far into the night. The pressure was increased by the constant press coverage of continuing developments, and by the uncomfortable feeling that many reporters knew much more about the facts than we did.

Within a few days, I was impressed because our offices were completely furnished with draperies. It was not my experience that government offices were equipped so nicely or so quickly, so I assumed that this was in some way a mark of the prestige of the Special Prosecutor.

A few days later, I was visited by an FBI agent who said he was our security officer. He informed me that the drapes were lined with a special sound-deadening material to prevent anyone from picking up conversations from outside the office by using a directional microphone. He also told me to keep the venetian blinds closed to obstruct the use of high-powered photography to read documents on our desks.

I was duly impressed. I recognized that these and other security measures were an effort to establish the credibility and professionalism of the Special Prosecutor's Office, and to prevent things like the public disclosure of grand jury testimony that had occurred in the original investigation of the Watergate burglary.

During the next week, one of the Washington papers carried the contents of two internal memoranda from the Special Prosecutor's Office, and my confidence in our security measures suddenly decreased. We discovered that the contents of our waste baskets were being picked up by some enterprising individual and sold to the newspaper. A shredder was promptly added to our office and used nightly thereafter.

My precise role had not been clearly defined when I began work. At first I was to be part of a "shadow" prosecution team that might be required to take over from the three assistant United States attorneys who had investigated and prosecuted the Watergate break-in case. They had moved into the Special Prosecutor's Office and were in charge of the investigation into the cover-up of the Watergate break-in. I was not very enthusiastic about such a tenuous relationship and mentioned my displeasure to Vorenberg.

However, my concern was relieved in an unexpected way. On June 21, the American Civil Liberties Union filed a brief in support of McCord's motion for a new trial, severely criticizing the original Watergate prosecutors and listing twenty-three areas in which they had failed to pursue the investigation and prosecute the case diligently. The subsequent publicity about these charges made the position of the three prosecutors with Cox untenable, and in order to prevent any embarrassment of the Special Prosecutor they resigned on June 29.

A few days later, the papers carried reports that the three original prosecutors had recommended indictments against H. R. Haldeman, John Ehrlichman, John Dean, and John Mitchell. Cox denounced the stories and characterized their source as a gross breach of professional ethics. He stated that no conclusion on who would be charged had been reached, and that such a decision would he made by him and his staff. He added that any member of his staff would be dismissed for commenting to the media on a proposed indictment. This was typical of Cox's high standards of professional ethics, his efforts to protect the rights of the individuals who were under investigation, and his constant concern about not jeopardizing future cases by adverse pretrial publicity.

As a result of the resignation of the original Watergate prosecutors, the Special Prosecutor formed his own task force to investigate and prosecute the Watergate cover-up. This group was headed by Jim Neal, who had been working on the cover-up since Cox had been appointed. It also resulted in a clarification of my role.

On June 29, I met with Vorenberg and Heyman and was asked if I would like to be in charge of an investigation into the Fielding break-in. I said I had heard of the Ellsberg break-in—the break-in at Ellsberg's psychiatrist's office—but that I did not know of any other break-in. Someone politely pointed out that Fielding was the name of Ellsberg's psychiatrist. I was told that it was not clear who was responsible for the break-in or whether it violated any federal statute, and that it would be up to me to develop these matters further. I agreed to review the relevant grand jury testimony and FBI interviews.

The somewhat limited file showed that Howard Hunt and Gordon Liddy had engineered a break-in during the Labor Day weekend of 1971 at the office of Dr. Lewis Fielding, a psychiatrist in Beverly Hills, California. Hunt, a former CIA agent, had been recruited for employment by Charles Colson, special counsel to the President. Liddy, a former FBI agent, had been recruited by Hunt. The purpose of the break-in was to obtain derogatory information about Daniel Ellsberg, a former patient of Dr. Fielding. Three months earlier, Ellsberg had been indicted for having unauthorized possession of classified government documents—documents which had been published in the Pentagon Papers. Any derogatory information obtained was to have been leaked to the press by Colson in order to discredit Ellsberg. The break-in appeared to have been recommended by Hunt and Liddy to Egil Krogh and David Young, who had been placed in charge of what was called the Special Investigations Unit by John Ehrlichman, the President's advisor for domestic affairs. The Unit operated out of Room 16 in the basement of the Executive Office Building, and as such was part of what was loosely referred to as the White House. It also appeared that Krogh and Young had obtained Ehrlichman's approval for the break-in, and that funds for the operation had been obtained by Colson in cash from a private individual and not government funds.

I found the file intriguing and challenging—it involved two of the President's top advisors, a possible violation of Ellsberg's right to a fair trial, the possible violation of Dr. Fielding's right to be free from unreasonable search and seizure as protected by the Fourth Amendment to the Constitution, and a potential test of the claim of national security as against the provisions of the Fourth Amendment. So on July 2, I agreed to be responsible for the investigation and the prosecution if it developed that we had a provable case. I was appointed head of a task force that also had responsibility for investigating any other break-ins by the Special Investigations Unit; evidence of possible abuse by the White House of the Internal Revenue Service, the FBI, and the CIA; and evidence of wiretaps authorized by the White House on certain newspaper reporters and others. Some time later, my task force was given responsibility for investigating any illegality in connection with the President's income-tax returns. The members of the task force were Nate Akerman (26), Phil Bakes (25), Charles Breyer (32), Henry Hecht (27), Jay Horowitz (30), and Frank Martin (26). Bakes and Breyer worked with me on the Fielding break-in; Horowitz was responsible for the other matters. Only two had prior prosecutorial experience—Breyer as an assistant prosecutor in San Francisco, and Horowitz as an assistant United States attorney in New York.

4

Investigation of the Fielding Break-In

We are involved here with the arrogance of unlimited power
of the President's staff.

—from the trial notes of William H. Merrill

As we began our investigation, various columnists were questioning
whether Nixon could continue as president. On July 6, 1973, in the
Washington Post, Marquis Childs wrote: "The issue is no longer
who is telling the truth and who is falsifying. The issue is whether President Nixon can govern the country for the next three years." In the same
issue, Stuart Alsop expressed similar thoughts under the title "A Paraplegic
Presidency."

It would have been unwise to call witnesses before the grand jury
immediately. Their testimony would be under oath, would be taken
down stenographically, and would have to be made available to the defendants prior to any trial. So first we had to learn, through informal office

interviews, each witness's involvement, the manner in which he might be expected to testify, and the extent to which his recollection of events might need reconstruction.

One of the first witnesses we interviewed was the person from whom Colson obtained $5,000 in cash that was used by Hunt and Liddy to cover their expenses for the break-in. His somewhat slick appearance and evasive manner of answering questions were such that I felt he would not make a good impression on the trial jury. After the interview was over, and in my enthusiasm that the investigation had begun, I almost shouted, "If he testifies, the defendants are dead!"

But we had only scratched the surface, and there was much more important work to do.

The first significant step was to interview David Young, the coleader of the Special Investigations Unit. It was Young who was apparently responsible for calling the group the Plumbers, because one of their purposes was to stop leaks to the press of information that Nixon felt involved national security.

Young had come to Washington as a member of Henry Kissinger's National Security Council after a few years with a large, prestigious New York law firm. He answered questions slowly and deliberately. In fact, he had such difficulty in answering questions directly, and gave such long, involved answers, that he always seemed to be hiding something.

When Young was interviewed by the original Watergate prosecutors, his attorney advised them that unless Young was granted immunity from prosecution, he would refuse to testify before the grand jury on the basis of the Fifth Amendment to the Constitution, which protected him from being forced to incriminate himself. In return for his request for immunity, he advised the prosecutors that Young had the only copy of a memo from himself and Krogh to Ehrlichman that authorized what occurred at Dr. Fielding's office. In the memo, dated August 11, 1971, Young and Krogh recommended "a covert operation to examine all the files still held by Ellsberg's psychoanalyst." This recommendation was followed by the words "Approve" and "Disapprove" with a black felt-tip pen. Ehrlichman had placed a check mark opposite "Approve" and had written, "If done under your assurance that it is not traceable."

This memo was so significant that the prosecutors applied to the court for immunity for Young, and it was granted in the early part of May 1973. When the memo was later made public during testimony before a Senate committee, the operation was given the "Good Housebreaking Seal of Approval" by Herblock in the July 25 issue of the *Washington Post*.

According to Young, he had this copy of the August 11 memo as a result of a rather unique chain of events. Near the end of April 1973, Ehrlichman asked Young to bring the Plumbers' files to his office for his review. Young did so, but only after making a copy of the August 11 memo for himself. A few days later, Young met with Ehrlichman to get the files back. At that meeting, during a discussion about the Fielding matter, Young said the files showed that Ehrlichman had authorized it. Young added that he always assumed that Ehrlichman had cleared it with "higher authority." Ehrlichman replied that "the memo was too sensitive to be kept in the file," and that Young should not question whether Ehrlichman had cleared the operation with any higher authority. When Young suggested that others might find out about the memo, Ehrlichman replied that they would have to take their chances on that. Ehrlichman added that if it happened, they would have to claim national security. When Young returned to his office with the files, he discovered that the August 11 memo had been removed.

We also obtained a copy of a memo from Young, dated August 27, that he had prepared for Ehrlichman, which Ehrlichman sent to Colson. The memo was entitled "Hunt/Liddy Special Project #1" and read: "On the assumption that the proposed undertaking by Hunt and Liddy would be carried out and would be successful, I would appreciate receiving from you by next Wednesday a game plan as to how and when you believe the materials should be used." When I interviewed Young in early July, I was shocked by the vagueness of his recollection about whether he and Krogh discussed with Ehrlichman the meaning of the term "covert operation," how they planned to "examine all the files," or what Ehrlichman meant by "not traceable." It was as though they had talked, but had not used words.

Instead, Young preferred to tell us that what had been done was justified on grounds of national security—and here he had no trouble with his recollection. According to Young, Ellsberg was a threat to national security. Young stated that Ellsberg's revelation of the Pentagon Papers had already damaged national security. He stressed that a copy of the Pentagon Papers had been delivered to the Russian Embassy. According to Young, Ellsberg was aware of other sensitive classified information involving national security, and he might be planning to release this too. Therefore, Young felt that an examination of Ellsberg's psychiatrist's file might reveal Ellsberg's past activities and future plans.

Young's reliance on national security was not very persuasive. Instead, it seemed to be a defense that was being used by him psychologically to excuse conduct that was wrong and prevent him from viewing his conduct objectively. For one thing, there was no mention of national security in the August 11 memo he and Krogh wrote to Ehrlichman. The memo implied only that information in Ellsberg's psychiatrist's file would be helpful to the CIA in coming up with a psychological profile on Ellsberg. If the Fielding break-in had really involved national security, then Ehrlichman (and indeed the President) should have known about it in advance. In addition, if there were a genuine concern about Ellsberg involving national security, then Young and Krogh should have applied through Ehrlichman to the Attorney General for a tap on Ellsberg's phone, as provided for by statute. Or they should have attempted to obtain the information from Dr. Fielding's files by applying to a judge for a search warrant. But they did neither. Finally, the national-security rationale for the break-in was inconsistent with the reason for seeing Ellsberg's psychiatrist's file first mentioned in an earlier memo from Howard Hunt. Hunt had said the file should be reviewed for any derogatory information about Ellsberg that could be used to destroy Ellsberg.

The alleged delivery of the Pentagon Papers to the Russian Embassy was a strange matter in itself. All reports from the FBI made it clear that there was no evidence to connect Ellsberg with it. In fact, there was no solid evidence that it really occurred. We speculated that it could have been engineered by Colson or the President in an effort to tar Ellsberg with the same brush Nixon had used on Alger Hiss. It also seemed part of a plan by the President to influence the Supreme Court in its consideration of the Pentagon Papers case. A news story by a reporter known to be the source of friendly leaks from the White House regarding such a delivery appeared on June 29—the day after Ellsberg was indicted, and three days after the Pentagon Papers case was argued before the Supreme Court.

When we questioned Hunt, we were aware that after he had been convicted for his part in the Watergate burglary, he had been granted immunity from any further Watergate prosecution. Thereafter, he had testified before the grand jury on several occasions, and it appeared that he had testified differently on certain occasions about the same events. We also learned during our interviews with him that it was not always easy to know whether he was telling the complete truth. The secret-agent mentality was so deeply imbedded in him that it was difficult to pry things out.

It appeared that Hunt was hired by Ehrlichman to work at the White House in early July 1971 on the recommendation of Charles Colson. Just prior to being hired, Colson had a telephone conversation with Hunt that Colson recorded. In this conversation, Colson expressed his dislike of Ellsberg, who had recently been indicted in connection with the Pentagon Papers. With Colson's encouragement, Hunt expressed a similar dislike of Ellsberg and agreed with Colson that Ellsberg should be "tried in the press."

Shortly thereafter, on July 20, 1971, Hunt became aware that two FBI agents called on Dr. Fielding in Beverly Hills, California, and asked if he would talk to them about a Daniel Ellsberg, his former patient. Fielding refused, because to do so would have violated the confidential relationship between patient and doctor that the law protects. A few days later, Hunt sent a memo to Colson in which he set forth several suggestions for obtaining information about Ellsberg in order to destroy his public image and credibility. One of the items listed in the memo was the examination of Ellsberg's psychiatric file. Colson sent the memo to Krogh and Young.

According to Hunt, he and Liddy met with Krogh and Young and recommended what Hunt said he was familiar with in the CIA as a "surreptitious entry" (and what Liddy said he was familiar with in the FBI as a "black bag job") into Dr. Fielding's office. This led to the August 11 memo from Krogh and Young to Ehrlichman.

Hunt also involved his former colleagues at the CIA. When he was hired at the White House, he told Colson he might need some help from the CIA. Colson repeated Hunt's request to Ehrlichman, and the day after Hunt was hired, Ehrlichman called General Robert Cushman, then deputy director of the CIA, and told Cushman to expect a call from Hunt and to provide him with whatever material he requested. In late July, Hunt met with Cushman and later received from the CIA false identification, a wig, a voice changer, a regular camera, and a camera concealed in a tobacco pouch.

Hunt also suggested to Krogh and Young that they have the CIA do a psychological profile on Ellsberg. Young followed up on this, and the CIA had provided such a profile just prior to the August 11 memo. The CIA was concerned about how the profile would be used. Young assured them that it would be done in a way that would not be attributable to the Agency.

In late August, Hunt and Liddy went to California to conduct preliminary surveillance of Dr. Fielding's office. During this trip, they took several pictures of the outside of Dr. Fielding's office building (one showing Dr. Fielding's car in the parking lot), which Hunt asked the CIA to develop when he and Liddy returned to Washington. On the day Hunt picked up the developed pictures, General Cushman called Ehrlichman and told him that the CIA could not provide any further help to Hunt, because Hunt was going beyond what had been originally contemplated.

After their return from the surveillance of Dr. Fielding's office, Hunt and Liddy prepared a memo regarding how they proposed to carry out the break-in. The memo was in great detail, including such matters as a layout of Dr. Fielding's office and an escape plan in case of detection—a 30-foot piece of nylon rope for sliding to the ground. Hunt told us that the original of that memo and the originals of the pictures he and Liddy had taken of Dr. Fielding's office were placed in the safe in his office at the White House. When Hunt's name surfaced in connection with the Watergate break-in in June 1972, the FBI opened Hunt's safe. The memo and the pictures were not there. We were never able to prove who removed and destroyed this evidence.

Hunt was also busy in another area. In late August he sent Ehrlichman a scurrilous, slanderous memo about one of Ellsberg's attorneys, characterizing him as a defender of traitors, thereby also damning Ellsberg. On August 24, Ehrlichman sent a memo to Colson that read: "The attached memorandum by Howard Hunt should be useful in connection with the recent request that we get something out on Ellsberg." A few days later, Colson gave Hunt's memo to a newspaper reporter. After his guilty plea in June 1974, Colson admitted that the "recent request" referred to in Ehrlichman's memo was from the President.

After Ehrlichman's approval of the August 11 memo and the surveillance trip, Hunt recruited Bernard Barker, Eugenio Martinez, and Felipe DeDiego, Cuban Americans whom Hunt had known when he had been involved in the Bay of Pigs invasion for the CIA. Barker, Martinez, and DeDiego were to make the examination of Dr. Fielding's records so that Hunt and Liddy would not be on the premises if anything went wrong. This was in order to comply with Ehrlichman's instruction that the operation be "not traceable." The examination itself was also to be concealed so as to be not traceable. The plan devised was that the Cuban Americans would wear delivery uniforms and bring a suitcase addressed to Dr. Fielding to his office. They would be let in by the cleaning personnel and would leave the suitcase (which contained black cloth for covering the windows, photographic equipment, rubber gloves, and the escape rope). On leaving the office and the building, they would push the lock-catch buttons so they could get in when they returned after the cleaning people had left. Unfortunately for them, the lock buttons were checked by the cleaning personnel and the doors were locked when the Cuban Americans returned, so they had to break the locks. They also had difficulty in communicating with Hunt and Liddy. The walkie-talkies Hunt had purchased in Chicago on the trip to the West Coast operated on the same frequency as one of the Los Angeles taxicab companies and therefore could not be used.

The interviews with Hunt led naturally to the CIA and Cushman, who by then was the commandant of the Marine Corps. We were also curious as to whether the CIA had any advance knowledge of the break-in at Dr. Fielding's office, why Cushman told Ehrlichman that the CIA would no longer help Hunt, and what investigation the CIA had made regarding Hunt's surveillance pictures. Cushman's name had also come up in connection with another aspect of our investigation. In December 1972, during the investigation into the Watergate burglary, the original Watergate prosecutors learned that Hunt had obtained some material from the CIA. After considerable effort, they managed to learn from William Colby, then deputy director of the CIA, that this assistance to Hunt had occurred after a phone call from Ehrlichman to Cushman in July 1971. Colby immediately advised Ehrlichman of this revelation. Ehrlichman then called Cushman and said he did not remember calling Cushman about Hunt. He suggested that Cushman prepare a memo about the matter and send him a copy. Cushman wrote such a memo in which he recited the fact that Hunt had been provided some assistance "after receiving a call from Ehrlichman, Colson or Dean." When Ehrlichman received a copy of this memo, he called Cushman and objected to the use of his name. Cushman prepared a new memo in which he stated that the call, which preceded the assistance to Hunt, "was from someone whose name I cannot recall."

By the time I met with Cushman in July 1973, we had obtained from the CIA a copy of the transcript of the meeting between Hunt and Cushman, which Cushman had recorded (without Hunt's knowledge). In the transcript, there were specific references to the call from Ehrlichman that had preceded the meeting. We were initially hampered in attempting to use the transcript because the CIA claimed that it had been discovered only within the last two months by a secretary who was cleaning out her desk. Later, it turned out to have been discovered several months earlier, and in fact had been shown to Cushman in December 1972 prior to the phone calls he received from Ehrlichman. This and other events caused me to wonder about the efficiency and veracity of the CIA.

After several attempts through his aide, a colonel, I finally arranged a meeting with Cushman at his office at the end of the day. Somehow my driver got lost, and by the time we found a telephone to get more exact directions, I was half an hour late—not a very auspicious way to start a meeting with the commandant of the Marine Corps.

The general had a clear recollection of his call to Ehrlichman in August 1971, when he had advised Ehrlichman that the CIA would not provide any further assistance to Hunt. However, Cushman adamantly maintained that he did not remember who had called him previously to request assistance for Hunt. He also contended that he did not believe Ehrlichman influenced him in any way in writing the memos in December 1972 about that call. Cushman stated that prior to his call to Ehrlichman in August 1971, he had not seen or heard about the pictures Hunt had taken of Dr. Fielding's office, which had been developed by the CIA. The general added that he was not aware of any effort by the CIA to check the license number of the car in one of those pictures (which was Dr. Fielding's car). Finally, General Cushman said he did not know of Young's request to the CIA for a psychological profile on Ellsberg at the time he told Ehrlichman that Hunt would get no more help from the CIA. Cushman's only explanation for cutting off Hunt was that Hunt had exceeded his original request by bringing another person (Liddy) into the situation.

Even to us amateurs on the Special Prosecutor's staff, the pictures of the building and Fielding's car looked like surveillance for surreptitious entry. It would have been easy for the CIA to have checked the ownership of the car from the license numbers in one of the pictures, and by August a check of the FBI indexes would have revealed that Dr. Fielding had been interviewed in connection with Daniel Ellsberg. I did not believe Cushman was telling me the truth, but rather than say so and lose any chance of cooperation, I suggested that he think about these matters further prior to being required to come before the grand jury to testify under oath.

During this time, former Attorney General Mitchell was appearing before the Ervin Committee. From his testimony, it appeared that one of the motives for the cover-up of the Watergate burglary was to prevent the public disclosure of the Fielding break-in. Mitchell's testimony about his role in the cover-up resulted in a devastating cartoon by Herblock in the July 12 issue of the *Washington Post* showing the former head of the Department of Justice trying to explain to the American people what he had done to the figure of Justice lying bleeding at his feet.

Because of Mitchell's testimony, I suggested to Henry Ruth, Cox's deputy special prosecutor, that we should consider the advisability of having the trial of the Fielding break-in before the trial of the Watergate cover-up. I recognized that the cover-up case was receiving far more publicity (because it might involve the President), and that my suggestion would be strongly resisted by the members of the cover-up task force. A few weeks later, I repeated this suggestion to Archie. He replied that I was an idealist—adding, "like I am."

Our eventual trial of the Fielding break-in also faced competition from another quarter. Shortly after Cox was appointed, the Los Angeles County district attorney told Cox he was interested in the Fielding break-in as a violation of the California burglary statute, and asked if this would interfere with any plans of the Special Prosecutor. Cox indicated that he did not have enough knowledge of the facts or the law to make a final decision, but that he would not want to prevent the district attorney from taking whatever action he felt was proper. So the Los Angeles district attorney immediately began calling witnesses before the county grand jury. After our investigation had proceeded for a few weeks, we became disturbed about the effect of a trial in the Los Angeles County Court. If the defendants were acquitted in California, this might make it impossible for us to obtain a conviction, or even go to trial. We felt that the federal constitutional issues involved in the break-in were far more important to the nation than a burglary case in California. We were also concerned that a county prosecutor would not have the same standing to meet the anticipated national-security defense that the Watergate Special Prosecutor had. So, we made several phone calls attempting to persuade the Los Angeles district attorney that he should not get himself in a position where his case came to trial first. In order to discuss this further, and in person, it was decided near the end of July that I should go to Los Angeles. Such a trip would also make it possible for me to visit the scene of the crime.

Just before I went to Los Angeles, I had lunch with an old Air Corps buddy who was an attorney for a government agency and whom I had not seen for twenty years. Much of our lunch was taken up with his plans for retirement in the near future. It was difficult for me to identify with such a discussion. I felt my professional life was just beginning—or at least it was beginning a new, exciting, and rewarding phase—and I was far removed from any thoughts of retirement.

5

Scene of the Crime

They say they did the thing that was more important to the country. Yet, in doing so, they were destroying the rights and liberties for which the Revolution was fought—for which men and women died. The rights and liberties upon which our Nation was founded and which make this Country important and different from most others.

—*from the trial notes of William H. Merrill*

My first impression of Dr. Fielding was that he was mild-mannered, gentle, and shy. Our initial meeting was in his attorney's office, and the doctor was obviously uncomfortable about the unpleasant prospect of more unwanted publicity. However, when I explained that we were interested in the constitutional ramifications of what appeared to be a gross abuse of government power, he seemed somewhat relieved and invited us to his own office.

Dr. Fielding had occupied the small, simple office with the same plain furniture on the second floor of a two-story office building on Bedford Drive for over twenty years. When he had been called to his office by the Beverly Hills Police on Labor Day weekend in 1971, he observed that his office door had been forced open, the lock on the wooden cabinet doors that covered his files had been broken, the locked file drawers were bent from being pried open, his desk drawers were open, and there were papers all over the floor. There were pills on the floor. One of the officers said it appeared someone was looking for drugs and that one of the offices on the first floor was in the same condition.

Dr. Fielding told me he had wanted to believe that the break-in was drug connected, but he could not. He remembered the indictment of Ellsberg in June, the visit of the two FBI agents and their questions about Ellsberg in July, and felt there must be some connection. He was more convinced this was so when one of the cleaning men told him about the delivery of the suitcase.

Despite his conviction that the break-in was related to Ellsberg, Dr. Fielding decided not to say anything to his former patient, because he felt Ellsberg had enough on his mind after his indictment. The doctor was also concerned that any publicity about the break-in would adversely affect his relationships with his patients, who then might wonder whether the office was bugged and be afraid that others would hear their intimate revelations.

I questioned Dr. Fielding about these matters later, before the grand jury in Washington. He recited them in detail, but in a rather cold, clinical manner. So I asked him to do what I was sure he often asked his patients to do: try to recapture the feelings he had as he viewed his office that day in 1971. The result was unexpected and very moving. He recounted his uneasy conviction that it was not a drug robbery but was related to Ellsberg, and that some papers regarding Ellsberg had been looked at. His testimony continued:

> FIELDING: I had the feeling that those papers particularly had been looked through thoroughly, so I had a rather total helpless feeling. I talked to my counsel and he said, 'There isn't anything you can do.' I thought about the police. I thought about my councilman. I thought about the mayor. I thought about the Governor—our Governor is Governor Reagan. I thought about possibly congressmen, senators. I thought, you know, if this thing has really been carried through as a follow-up to the FBI

refusal, my refusal to talk with them, then I thought it must be carried on from pretty high places and there really isn't anything I can do about it.

I must say it disheartened me and discouraged me. It left me with a sinking feeling.

MERRILL: With a what?

FIELDING: With a rather sinking feeling. I put well over four and a half years of my life shortly after I graduated from medical school in the Army and was with the Third Army with Patton's Army, went with a little old evacuation hospital with every important division that operated through there, through France, Germany, and Austria, have all five battle stars, you know, and I knew what it was about and what it was for, and I thought, you know, have we come to that kind of a pass where a man's office can be . . . Excuse me.

With that, the doctor lost his composure and broke down momentarily. My eyes were not the only wet ones in the room as I continued:

MERRILL: I think we all appreciate how you feel. That is why we are here.

FIELDING: Yes. I really didn't want to believe that, you know, I didn't want to believe it was possible that a man's office could just be entered on the word of someone high up and myself be unable to do anything about it.

After talking with Dr. Fielding, we met the Beverly Hills police officers who were at the doctor's office as a result of the break-in. Then I interviewed the attorney who had been in charge of the Ellsberg trial and who was in private practice in San Diego. I was convinced that he had been unaware of the break-in until it was disclosed to him by his superiors in Washington in April 1973.

While in Los Angeles, I also had to continue our dialogue with the Los Angeles district attorney. I met with him, and with his assistants who were handling the burglary case. They seemed to recognize the paramount nature of the constitutional issues involved in our case and our greater ability to deal with the problem of national security. They also recognized the difficulty we would face if they lost their case. However, they were concerned that we might not have the facts to support our legal theory, so they did not want to drop their case only to find out later that we had no case. At that time, I could not give them any assurance as to the soundness of our case, so we agreed to keep the lines of communication open in an effort to resolve our problem in a mutually satisfactory manner in the future.

One final, delicate matter that had to be accomplished in Los Angeles was an interview with Judge Matthew Byrne, the federal judge who had been in charge of the Ellsberg trial. This interview was necessary because on April 30, the *Washington Star* carried a story that there had been a meeting between Nixon and Judge Byrne at San Clemente at which Judge Byrne might have been offered the job of director of the FBI. That same day, in commenting on the newspaper story, Judge Byrne admitted meeting with Ehrlichman and Nixon on April 5, at which time Ehrlichman suggested that the President was interested in appointing Byrne head of the FBI.

During our meeting, Judge Byrne strongly maintained that he did not believe Ehrlichman's offer was an attempt to influence him in the Ellsberg case. I never became aware of any evidence to dispute this. However, I felt that Ehrlichman's offer was the first step in an effort by the President to persuade Judge Byrne not to reveal publicly the Fielding break-in.

This belief was based on many facts. Hunt and Liddy's involvement in the Fielding break-in was revealed to Robert Mardian immediately after the arrests in June 1972 for the Watergate break-in. Mardian was an assistant attorney general, and later one of the convicted defendants in the Watergate cover-up case. Near the end of March 1973, Ehrlichman told Young that he was concerned that Hunt might reveal the Fielding break-in to the grand jury. In early April, Ehrlichman and Nixon were concerned that Dean might talk to the original Watergate prosecutors. On April 15, Dean in fact did reveal the occurrence of the Fielding break-in, and Hunt and Liddy's part in it, to the prosecutors. The information was then reported to Henry Peterson, head of the Criminal Division of the Department of Justice, and by him to the President on April 18. For a week, the President refused to allow the information to be transmitted to Los Angeles for revelation to Judge Byrne. Nixon relented and allowed the information to be sent to the judge only after Peterson and Attorney General Kleindienst threatened to resign.

From all of this, I felt certain that the Fielding break-in was discussed with the President by Mitchell in June 1972, and by in March or early April 1973. I believed that Ehrlichman's call to Judge Byrne was at the President's direction, and that it was the first step in an effort by Nixon to persuade the judge that the Fielding break-in should not be made public.

6

The Grand Jury

"This concept of 'national defense' cannot be deemed an end in itself, justifying any . . . power designed to promote such a goal. Implicit in the term 'national defense' is the notion of defending those values and ideas which set this nation apart. It would indeed be ironic if, in the name of national defense, we would sanction the subversion of those liberties which make the defense of the Nation worthwhile."

—*Justice Earl Warren, 1967, as quoted from*
the trial notes of William H. Merrill

August and September were taken up with interviewing and questioning, before the grand jury, thirty witnesses connected with the Fielding break-in. The grand jury is an ancient institution, having come down to us through eight hundred years of development under English Common Law:

At first the ancient grand jury was made up of twelve knights or other freemen of every "hundred," a territorial division within the English county. The ancient English constitutions of Clarendon, 1164 A.D., declared that "if such men were suspected whom none wished or dared to accuse, the sheriff, being thereto required by the bishop, should swear twelve men of the neighborhood, or village, to declare the truth" with regard to a supposed crime in the community. They were summoned in the capacity of accusers or witnesses rather than as judges, and it was at this time that the grand jury was first established or else reorganized in a way such that we are able to recognize it as being related to the grand juries sitting in our state and federal courts. (Hon. Irving R. Kaufman, "The Grand Jury—Its Role and Its Powers," 17 Federal Rules Decisions 331)

During its history, the grand jury protected citizens from being unjustly charged by the king with having committed a crime, and this protection is carried over into the federal system by Article V of the Bill of Rights, which provides that the grand jury is the only means by which federal felony charges can be brought.

There are some who criticize the grand jury system because an unscrupulous prosecutor can abuse the rights of a citizen by using the power of the grand jury unfairly. That power rests in the grand jury's right to compel witnesses to appear by subpoena, to question them under oath without their attorney being present in the grand jury room, and to bring criminal charges by means of an indictment.

The Watergate Special Prosecution Force was conscious that it might be the target of similar criticism for its use of the grand jury. Accordingly, we carefully tried to protect fully the rights of witnesses and potential defendants, particularly because of the notoriety of many of those who appeared before the grand jury. All the proceedings were taken down in shorthand by court reporters, with the recognition that they would undoubtedly be made public and reviewed by some judge at a later date.

We questioned Dr. Fielding, as described in chapter 5. Hunt was questioned about the planning of the operation and the assistance he had received from the CIA. Young was questioned about the planning, the obtaining of Ehrlichman's approval, and Ehrlichman's removal of memos from the file. Former Attorney General Kleindienst, Assistant Attorney General Peterson, former Assistant Attorney General Mardian, and three other Justice Department attorneys were questioned about the Pentagon Papers, Ellsberg, and other matters that might involve national security. We questioned General Cushman regarding his telephone calls with Ehrlichman about Hunt. There were eight other CIA employees we questioned regarding the assistance the Agency provided to Hunt, and the psychological profile of Daniel Ellsberg. Judge Byrne testified regarding his discussions with Ehrlichman about the directorship of the FBI. There were several witnesses who were questioned about providing and repaying the $5,000 that Ehrlichman requested from Colson. We also questioned several secretaries who had worked at the White House. Finally, we used grand jury subpoenas to obtain long-distance telephone records and copies of hotel registration cards and airplane tickets used by Hunt, Liddy, Barker, Martinez, and DeDiego.

Although it is not customary to call prospective defendants before the grand jury, we extended the opportunity of appearing before the grand jury to the prospective defendants in the Fielding case. It was accepted by all but Liddy. After Colson had been questioned for several days, his attorney said he did not want to continue, and if required to do so would take the Fifth Amendment. However, he was concerned that doing this might prejudice the grand jury against his client. In order to prevent any such prejudice, I requested a letter confirming that Colson would "take the Fifth." Then I told the grand jury that Colson had decided he did not want to testify any further, that he had the right to do this, and that they should not let this prejudice them against Colson. I did not tell them he would have refused to testify and would have pled the Fifth Amendment.

Ehrlichman testified without any unusual incident. He had been described by Joseph Kraft in the July 26, 1973, issue of the *Washington Post,* during his testimony before the Ervin Committee, as expressing "the corruption of power," and as "a man of maniacal arrogance." He did not give the same impression to the grand jury. Not that he was humble—I don't think Ehrlichman could ever be humble. He just was not arrogant. After his testimony was concluded, Bakes commented to me that under different circumstances, Ehrlichman would be "a neat guy to go on a camping trip with."

Ehrlichman apparently believed he could explain his way out of the seemingly incriminating evidence, but in his twisting and turning, he was often confronted with facts to which he could only reply that he did not remember. This made it seem like he had a very selective memory—remembering only those things that were harmless. In this respect he was different from Haldeman, who consistently answered that he did not remember. Of the two, Haldeman seemed much colder and calculating, and potentially far more dangerous where the rights of others were concerned.

Despite our efforts to be fair but firm with the witnesses, particularly the prospective defendants, there was some criticism in the press of our use of the grand jury. I suspected that it was the result of efforts by Pat Buchanan, the White House hatchet man. I also recognized that it was inevitable. We were forcing some of the most powerful men in the government to appear before us, to answer difficult and often embarrassing questions, and to explain their answers to our satisfaction. This was something they had not previously been compelled to do in their governmental careers.

Perhaps our greatest effort to avoid abuse of the grand jury was in the standard we used for the return of an indictment. As every TV viewer knows, the trial jury can find a defendant guilty only if all twelve members are convinced of that guilt "beyond a reasonable doubt." The grand jury, however, can charge a defendant with a crime, by returning an indictment, if a majority of the twenty-three members "have reasonable cause to believe that a crime was committed and that the defendant charged committed that crime." There is obviously considerable difference between "beyond a reasonable doubt" and "reasonable cause to believe." It is, therefore, much easier to have an indictment returned than it is to obtain a conviction.

So, in order to protect persons from being unfairly charged with a crime, a conscientious prosecutor should honestly believe there is enough evidence to convict beyond a reasonable doubt before he asks the grand jury to return an indictment. The Watergate Special Prosecution Force went even further.

We realized that we were dealing with men who had held the highest positions of responsibility in our government, and we felt that we had an obligation to them, as well as to the country, not to bring charges against them unless we believed that we would not only convict them but also sustain those convictions on appeal. In order to accomplish this, the Fielding break-in task force had many long, spirited sessions with Archie, much like high-level legal seminars, during which we discussed the facts we had developed and the law applicable to those facts. The discussion of the law included every major Supreme Court case on the complicated legal issues involved in obstruction of justice, specific intent to deprive a person of his civil rights, and the uncharted areas between protecting national security and preserving freedom.

During this period, strange feelings of sadness pervaded all our work. Most of the staff had been exposed to the political process enough to recognize how difficult it sometimes was to distinguish between loyalty and impropriety. So as the various individuals involved came through our offices, we tried not to sit in judgment of them. We felt the reality of the expression, "There but for the grace of God go I." Instead, there was a sense of regret about what we had to do. For my part, however, these same feelings did not exist for the President. Within the first few months, I felt that if what we had discovered was typical of what had occurred, and if it could be made public, then the President would (and should) be impeached. The anguish he had caused others and his continued deception of the public were too much for me to feel any regret about what would happen to him.

We felt we were dealing with the tenuous thread from which a free society hangs, with the problem of how a free society keeps itself free—free from those who would change it, and free from those who would protect it. The press helped in constantly keeping this before the public, and in so doing buoyed our morale. Illustrative of this was Joseph Kraft's column in the Sunday, August 19, issue of the *Washington Post:*

> The President wants Watergate to go away so he can get on with "matters of far greater importance." Like, for instance, what?
>
> The fact is that the world and the country are enjoying a period of relative calm. No business before the American people is anywhere near as important as achieving honest government which is what Watergate is all about. . . .

Watergate is by far the most portentous event now going. It has to do with the nature of the modern presidency and the relations between the executive and the other branches of government. It involves building trust between the President and the people. It concerns honest government, which is the basis of legitimacy in this country.

So to talk of moving from Watergate to more important problems is to stand the world on its head. The true danger is that the problem of honest government will not receive the careful attention it deserves from a country obsessed by the myth of world leadership and mired in the illusion of presidential power.

By coincidence, that same day Bishop Walker preached a sermon at Washington Cathedral about how the people seemed to want a king, and the dangers to a free society inherent in such longings.

That Sunday's *Post* also had a humorous yet frightening article by Philip Roth entitled "Nixon's Next Speech?" In it, the President supposedly has just been impeached and is congratulating the House and Senate for doing their job as they saw it: "That is what is known as separation of powers." He even applauds the members of his own party who voted against him as a vigorous and reassuring sign of their independence "which can only strengthen the democratic process here at home and enhance the image of American democracy abroad." However, since the separation of powers gives the executive branch an equal voice in the government, and the President has the sole responsibility for safeguarding the security of the nation, "I have decided tonight, to remain in this office" so as not to have failed those who voted him into that office. Although the easier choice would be to retire to San Clemente, he is not a quitter, and "In order to discourage those who would resort to violence of any kind, in order to maintain law and order in the nation and to safeguard the welfare and well-being of law-abiding American citizens, I have tonight, in my constitutional role as Commander-in-Chief, ordered the Joint Chiefs of Staff to place the Armed Forces on a stand-by alert around the nation . . . God bless each and every one of you. Good night."

An editorial in the *Washington Post* on August 28 entitled "Governments 'Black Bag' Jobs" put the issue more starkly with respect to the Fielding break-in:

> People seem to yearn for silver Watergate linings these days and to stretch pretty hard for them. But President Nixon may well have done the nation a good turn at his press conference last week when he opened up the question of burglaries in the national interest. . . .
>
> The people now talking cautiously to newspapers say that the FBI began edging into the national security burglary business back in the late 1930s as the nation moved closer to World War II.
>
> But, the path from the German consulates in the late 1930s and the early 1940s to the office in Los Angeles where Dr. Lewis Fielding practiced psychiatry in 1971 is long and disquieting.
>
> The only common thread between the burglary of an enemy office in order to gain information to break a war-time code and the entry into Dr. Fielding's office to get information on Daniel Ellsberg is that 1) both were burglaries and 2) both were justified in the name of national security. The problem is that somewhere along the line a lot of people neglected to draw the line between what constitutes a legitimate national security concern and what constitutes a blatant and mindless violation of the rights of an American citizen.

One of my clearest memories of the evils of the national-security mentality is when Archie and I met with several of the top internal security agents in the FBI to learn more about the so-called Kissinger wiretaps. We wanted to know who authorized the taps and what the national-security justification was, but they were resisting and desperately avoiding complete and full answers to our questions. Finally, the head of the FBI Internal Security Division got up from the conference table and went over to his couch, saying, "Let me show you what I mean." There on an end table was a set of scales with a little doll on each scale. I sat incredulous as he described one doll, dressed in Chinese costume, as China; the other, dressed in Russian costume, as Russia; and the eagle at the fulcrum as America. With frighteningly simplistic logic, he concluded the meeting by saying, "America is in the middle and must keep the balance. If the balance is ever tipped in favor of Russia or China, it will be the end of America."

In the evenings, I went for long walks as a physical break from the mental concentration. One night I walked to the Jefferson Memorial. Although it was after eleven when I arrived, I was amazed at how many tourists were still there. It seemed to be a good sign for the future of the country. As I stood and looked at the simple, majestic beauty of Jefferson's statue and the surrounding columns, I thought not only of the past and the principles that Jefferson and the others had established, but also wondered about the future and how what we were doing would be judged.

I talked about these principles one day to Bernard Barker in a cell at the Montgomery County Jail. He had been transferred there from a federal prison in Connecticut, where he was serving his sentence for the Watergate break-in. It was prior to his appearance before the grand jury, and I saw him with the approval of his attorney. I wanted to explore the possibility of convincing him to plead guilty to the Fielding break-in. Barker expressed bitterness about being considered a criminal. He said he had a real-estate business in Miami and a good reputation as a law-abiding citizen. When I asked him what he would have felt if someone had broken into his real-estate office, he replied that he had thought about that when they were breaking into the office in California and it bothered him. This seemed to be an opening, so I asked him about my understanding that he had been forced to flee Cuba to save his life, and about his subsequent efforts to overthrow Castro in order to return freedom to his people. When I pointed out that what he had done to Dr. Fielding was similar to what he objected to and fought against in Castro's Cuba, tears came to his eyes, and he acknowledged that his daughter said the same things to him. I felt as though I had brought Barker a long way down the road to admitting to the grand jury that what he had done was wrong, but the psychological block was too strong and he was never able to make that final step.

We had very sophisticated equipment to protect the secrecy of the grand jury proceedings. There was a unique alarm system that would go off at night simply by the vibration of anyone walking in the room, and the door to the grand jury room had special locks. The latter caused us some trouble one afternoon when the deputy marshal on duty pushed the wrong button at lunchtime and locked everyone out. We had several witnesses waiting to testify and twenty-three impatient grand jurors. My frustration increased when I had trouble trying to persuade our FBI security officer to leave whatever he was doing and bring the only key over to the courthouse so we could get into the room. However, in a few minutes I heard a cheer, and the grand jurors filed past the metal-detector device and into the grand jury room. Chuck Breyer had opened the door with a coat hanger.

The grand jury proved to be the opening wedge into the national-security armor of those involved in the Fielding break-in. By early October, our investigation had proceeded to the point where we had sufficient evidence to prove that Egil Krogh, the coauthor of the August 11 break-in memo to Ehrlichman, had committed perjury when he first testified before the grand jury prior to the appointment of Cox. However, we did not feel we had sufficient evidence about the break-in. Our dilemma was whether to immediately indict Krogh for perjury, or wait and combine the perjury charges against Krogh with charges relating to the break-in when that indictment was finally returned.

After several discussions, we decided there would be many tactical advantages in charging Krogh with perjury first. Krogh would be alone, without the psychological comfort of other defendants. The perjury case would be much simpler if it were not combined with the break-in. It would be much more difficult for Krogh to raise the national-security defense against the perjury charge. We felt that Krogh's fear of a perjury conviction (as an attorney he would probably face permanent disbarment) might influence him to plead guilty to the break-in. We also felt we had Krogh's conscience working for us. Finally, it would be the Watergate Special Prosecution Force's first indictment. So, on October 11, the day after Vice President Agnew resigned, we indicted Krogh for perjury. However, before we could explore his conscience further, we had to live through the firestorm of October 20.

7

The Saturday Night Massacre

"Ultimately no nation can be great unless its greatness is laid on foundations of righteousness and decency."

—*President Theodore Roosevelt, 1899, as quoted from the trial notes of William H. Merrill*

The confrontation between Cox and the President began building soon after Cox was appointed. We never received cooperation from the White House in response to our requests for documents and files, which for the Fielding break-in started in the middle of August. Also, when we attempted to get information from the Treasury Department regarding Secret Service wiretaps, we met with resistance that seemed to have been orchestrated by the White House.

A prediction of the showdown over the presidential tapes was made by Evans and Novak in the *Washington Post* on July 19, suggesting that Cox would resign if the President refused to produce the tapes. Archie's reaction to the article was to circulate a memo which stated:

Despite Evans and Novak, all of you should resign yourselves to the fact that I am resigned to staying in office.

Updating your resumes is therefore a needless act.

On July 23, the President refused to relinquish the tapes, and Archie publicly announced his intention to subpoena them. As the dispute over the tapes continued and the pressure increased, I was so immersed in the investigation of the Fielding break-in that I did not completely recognize the consequences until the break with the President actually occurred. Cox issued a subpoena for certain tapes that he felt contained evidence of the Watergate cover-up. Nixon's lawyers objected, but Judge Sirica ordered compliance with the subpoena. Sirica's order was appealed. The Court of Appeals rejected the President's arguments of executive privilege and upheld Judge Sirica's order.

On October 19, John Dean pled guilty to conspiring to obstruct justice by covering up evidence related to the Watergate break-in. Whether the President's strategy was influenced by Dean's plea we may never know, but later that day Nixon announced he would give the court and the Senate Watergate Committee a summary of his tapes. He added that he had ordered Cox to cease his attempts to obtain the tapes by subpoena. The press reported that Cox would not obey the President's order. He was quoted as saying: "For me to comply with those instructions would violate my solemn pledge to the country to challenge exaggerated claims of executive privilege. I shall not violate my promise."

The next morning, most of the staff sensed we were on the verge of some major development and came into the office to see if there was anything we could do. We learned that Archie was going to have a press conference and we tried to draft various ideas for him to cover, but soon he asked to be left alone in his office to put his own thoughts on paper.

In his press conference, Archie said he would not cease his efforts to obtain the tapes. Even after the press conference, when we returned to our offices, there was no certainty about what would happen, and Archie laughed as he said, "Well, I might not be here Monday."

That evening, as I left my apartment for dinner at a friend's, I was suddenly struck by the possibility that the White House might take over the Special Prosecutor's Office. I felt that if this occurred, my prosecution memo on the Fielding break-in and a memo I had prepared on evidence relating to the President would never see the light of day. So, I stopped at our offices and picked up my copies of these memos. An hour later, I learned that Cox had been fired, and that the FBI had sealed off our offices and would not let anyone take anything out, even personal papers.

When the dinner ended and the other guests had left, I told my host about the documents I had, and of my concern they be kept out of the hands of the White House. He suggested that we go to his law office downtown and make copies, which he would then place in a safe-deposit box. In view of what had occurred, we felt the FBI might have gone to my apartment to see if I had any files at home, and not finding me, might be looking for my car. Therefore, my friend suggested that I park on a side street away from the entrance to his office building. As I walked from my car, the idea that I felt it was necessary to hide from my own government seemed so incredible that it was difficult to believe it was actually happening. When I returned to my apartment after copying the memos, I was relieved that there were no FBI agents waiting for me.

Sending the FBI to the already adequately guarded Special Prosecutor's Office seemed like a police-state maneuver, typical of what we had begun to expect from Nixon. To many of the younger attorneys, it was a confirmation of the fears they had previously expressed: if we got too close to the President, we would end up in a concentration camp. It also typified the manner in which the White House had previously forced various governmental agencies to do things that those involved recognized were wrong.

One of the agents sent to our offices had for several weeks worked closely with one of the members of my task force—Phil Bakes. When Bakes went to the office immediately after Cox was fired and saw the FBI agent he had been working with, he shouted in disbelief at how the agent could betray us. The agent shouted back, and in a few moments both men were in tears.

That Sunday, the *Washington Post* editorial was entitled "Justice Un-done." The *New York Times* editorial was entitled "One-Man Law," and Anthony Lewis's column was headed "The End Begins." In the October 26 issue of the *Washington Star*, Carl Rowan's column was entitled "Has President Nixon Gone Crazy?" The Sunday, October 28, issue of the *Washington Post* contained several disparaging cartoons about the situation.

Although the President's arbitrary action seemed to have tarnished the beauty of Washington for me, that Sunday I went for a walk around Roosevelt Island. The words carved in stone behind T.R.'s statue seemed so appropriate to the events we were dealing with: "Ultimately, no nation can be great unless its greatness is laid on foundations of righteousness and decency." With tragic results, the qualities of righteousness and decency had not been present at the Nixon White House.

The August issue of the *Atlantic* contained an article entitled "The Runaway Presidency" in which Arthur Schlesinger Jr. wrote: "Watergate is potentially the best thing to have happened to the presidency in a long time. If the trails are followed to their end, many, many years will pass before another White House staff dares to take the liberties with the Constitution and the laws the Nixon White House has taken."

The outcome was not immediately clear to Cox's leaderless staff. We all respected and admired Archie. There was almost a son–father relationship toward him by the younger lawyers, many of whom had been his students in law school. The younger lawyers were disappointed and disillusioned and believed the momentum of our investigations could never be revived. Immediately after Cox was fired, many of the younger lawyers favored group resignation as a protest over the firing, but gradually they realized that this might be just what Nixon wanted. They recognized that their successors might not be as sympathetic to an objective investigation, or that even if they were, it would take several weeks to catch up to the point where we were in understanding the facts and developing relationships with witnesses.

Our first discussion about what to do was held in another building because we were afraid the White House had ordered the FBI to bug our offices. During one of our meetings, I remember saying that we were up against a tough son-of-a-bitch and that if we were going to be successful, we would have to be just as tough. I also remember Jim Vorenberg saying that anyone who stayed had to be able to accept the risk of betrayal again. In the end, everyone agreed to stay as long as we could be assured that our investigations would be allowed to continue with objectivity and independence.

I have always believed that when the President fired Cox, he thought he had also fired all of the staff. He said he was abolishing the office of the Watergate Prosecutor. However, the employment of the individual members of the staff continued, almost incidentally, as the result of a conversation between Henry Ruth and Acting Attorney General Bork on Sunday. Ruth stated he presumed that we would now be working for the Department of Justice, and Bork agreed. On Monday morning, when the President realized we were still at work, there had been such a storm of protest, including suggestions of impeachment, that it was too late for Nixon to risk even greater furor by dismissing us.

When Archie came in to say goodbye on Tuesday, there were many tears. Although I felt he had been treated unjustly by Nixon and would miss him, I was not as affected as others. I remembered that under far more tragic circumstances, I had previously lived through the loss of two leaders, both of whom were buried in Arlington Cemetery.

Over the next few days, I met with Bork and Henry Peterson, head of the Criminal Division of the Department of Justice, regarding the Fielding break-in. From these meetings, I was convinced that they wanted us to continue the investigation objectively and independently. Bork even put himself out on a limb by signing a letter to the White House, which we had been preparing for Archie, demanding the production of certain documents and files.

Our first meeting with Jaworski was on Monday, November 5. There was much uneasiness on both sides, but I was immediately impressed by Leon's genuine desire to have the entire staff continue the investigations with complete independence.

In the November 6 issue of the *Washington Post,* Evans and Novak stated that the White House hoped that Jaworski would restrict our investigation of the Plumbers and fire me. They wrote: "Nothing has dismayed the White House more than the aggressive investigation of the plumbers by the Cox task force . . . Nixon aides believe Merrill's investigation . . . intends to implicate Mr. Nixon himself." I was said to be "an implacable foe of the President."

On Wednesday, November 7, Leon met with my task force and reviewed the evidence on the Fielding break-in. When the discussion of the evidence was ended, he said, "Okay, let's go get 'em." Leon was reacting as the experienced trial lawyer he was. The days of legal seminars were over. On Thursday, Leon sent a further letter to the White House demanding additional documents. In firing Cox and appointing Jaworski, Nixon had made the wrong moves again, and I was not to return to Detroit as quickly as the White House hoped.

8

Krogh Pleads Guilty

They would put national security above the Constitution—
above the law. The Constitution protects the people from such
a Government—they would protect the government from the
people. They put *themselves* above the law—and would be
answerable to no one.

—from the trial notes of William H. Merrill

In early May 1973, Egil Krogh had filed an affidavit with Judge Byrne
in which he claimed full responsibility for the Fielding break-in. As
we began our investigation, Krogh's affidavit appeared to be an effort
to protect Ehrlichman. This seemed natural since Krogh and Ehrlichman
were Christian Scientists, their families were close, Ehrlichman had advised
Krogh on college and law school, Krogh had clerked with Ehrlichman's law
firm in Seattle while he was in law school and joined the firm after gradu-
ation, and Ehrlichman had brought Krogh to Washington in 1968 as his
assistant in the White House when Nixon was elected.

It was conceivable that Krogh also might be trying to protect the President. We knew that Krogh had met with Nixon on July 24, 1971, and had
been told to find out all he could about Ellsberg. But we were concerned

about the possible truth of Krogh's affidavit because of his good reputation. He was often referred to as "Straight Arrow."

We also knew that Krogh had been bothered about the break-in from the time Hunt and Liddy returned from California and showed him pictures of Dr. Fielding's office that had been taken by Barker, Martinez, and DeDiego. No longer could he think of it as a "covert operation," in the cold, impersonal words of the August 11 memo, but he could now see, and remember each night as he fell asleep, the physical damage that had been done to the office of an American citizen. This undoubtedly led Krogh to turn down Hunt and Liddy's proposal that they break into Dr. Fielding's home after they had failed to find any information about Ellsberg in the doctor's office.

We decided to use Krogh's reputation and conscience to our advantage. The first step was taken in October 1973 when we charged him with perjury. The false testimony consisted of answers in which he denied knowing of any trips by Hunt and Liddy to California.

Krogh and his attorney, Steve Shulman, were stunned by our strategy to charge Krogh just with perjury. They were made even more uneasy by Judge Gesell's forceful statements about an early trial at Krogh's arraignment on October 18.

Shulman tried to avoid the impending disaster to his client by filing motions in which he claimed that if Krogh perjured himself, it was justified on grounds of national security. During the hearing on these motions on October 13, the judge clearly indicated his disagreement with Krogh's position, describing it once as a "Nuremberg defense." We kept up the pressure by sending our list of witnesses to Krogh's attorney on October 14. On October 15, Judge Gesell issued his opinion denying Krogh's motions.

After receiving the judge's opinion, I walked to lunch through McPherson Park across K Street from our offices. The temperature was around 80° and many people were eating lunch in the park. I noticed John Dean and several of our attorneys sitting on the grass eating sandwiches, and thought of the paradox between that picnic scene and the momentous issues with which we were struggling.

After Judge Gesell's ruling, we intensified our efforts to persuade Krogh to plead guilty to the break-in. The possibility of such a plea seemed real because Shulman had told us that Krogh now believed that what had been done was wrong.

We were far more interested in a guilty plea to the break-in than a perjury conviction. Such a plea would have much greater ramifications in support of the constitutional principles involved. It would make no difference in the possible sentence, since the civil-rights statute under which the break-in charge would be brought carried a maximum ten-year jail sentence, while each of the perjury charges carried five-year maximum jail sentences.

On October 19, I arranged a meeting of Krogh and Shulman with Jaworski. After discussing the certainty of a conviction for perjury and the fact that it would probably result in permanent disbarment, I described the benefits of a guilty plea to the break-in. I suggested that such a plea might be a means of avoiding permanent disbarment; it would eliminate the expense and emotional strain of two trials, because we would dismiss the perjury charges; it would provide Krogh with an opportunity for psychological purging; and most importantly, it would be beneficial to the country by helping prevent such improper activity in the future. In connection with the last suggestion, I stated that if Krogh now really believed the break-in was wrong, then he was morally obligated to plead guilty and make some public statement to that effect. I stressed that this was the only way Krogh could help prevent such conduct in the future. He could not help if he was tried and convicted, nor could he help if he was acquitted.

Leon mentioned an analogy between present events and those he was involved with during his service as a prosecutor at the Nuremberg Trials. Krogh seemed moved by this. Throughout the meeting, I was impressed by Krogh's composure.

The next week, I had further discussions with Shulman in which he said Krogh would plead to a misdemeanor (one-year maximum sentence). I replied that we felt the break-in was far too serious to accept a misdemeanor plea.

Early in the week, Judge Gesell set December 1 for the trial.

Shulman asked if we would agree not to question Krogh until after he was sentenced, and whether he would face any further prosecution in California (for the burglary charges) if he pled guilty. I discussed these matters with Jaworski and the Los Angeles district attorney and then informed Shulman that there would be no problem.

The next day Krogh agreed to plead to the break-in, and with Judge Gesell's help was persuaded to do so immediately rather than wait for the trial date.

On November 30, Krogh appeared before a packed courtroom. After pleading guilty, he made a statement that should help prevent many of the improprieties and agonies we include in the term "Watergate," particularly a citizen's right to be free from unreasonable search and seizure by his own government. He said:

> The sole basis for my defense was to have been that I acted in the interest of national security. However, upon serious and lengthy reflection, I now feel that the sincerity of my motivation cannot justify what was done and that I cannot in conscience assert national security as a defense. I am, therefore, pleading guilty because I have no defense to this charge. I will make a detailed statement as to my reasons which I will submit to the Court and make public prior to sentencing.
>
> My decision is based upon what I think and feel is right and what I consider to be the best interests of the nation. The values expressed by your Honor in the hearing on defense motions on November 13 particularly brought home to me the transcendent importance of the rule of law over the motivations of man.
>
> I have expressed to the Special Prosecutor's office my desire that I not be required to testify in this area until after sentencing. My plea today is based on conscience, and I want to avoid any possible suggestion that I am seeking leniency through testifying. The Special Prosecutor's office has expressed no objection to this position.
>
> My coming to this point today stems from my asking myself what ideas I wanted to stand for, what I wanted to represent to myself and to

my family and to be identified with for the rest of my experience. I simply feel that what was done in the Ellsberg operation was in violation of what I perceive to be a fundamental idea in the character of this country—the paramount importance of the rights of the individual. I don't want to be associated with that violation any longer by attempting to defend it.

In the December 10 issue of *Time,* the headline for the story about Krogh's plea was "The Fuse Burns Ever Closer."

On January 24, 1974, Krogh was sentenced from two to six years in prison, all but six months of which was suspended. He began serving his sentence on February 4.

9

The Indictment

We don't have a king. We overthrew a king, one who was not concerned with the rights of individuals. Yet, they acted as though they thought we had a king, and that he and they were above the law.

—*from the trial notes of William H. Merrill*

B y the first week of September 1973, we felt we were close to returning an indictment in the Fielding break-in case. In fact when Colson's attorney, concerned about his client's appearance before the Ervin Committee, asked about the indictment, I replied that it might be in a few days. However, the indictment was not presented to the grand jury until March 1974. The delay was caused by many things: concern about the sufficiency of the facts we had developed before the grand jury, further legal analysis of the violation to be charged, the decision to indict Krogh for perjury first, the firing of Cox, preparing for Krogh's perjury trial, waiting to question Krogh after his guilty plea until he was sentenced in January, negotiating with Ehrlichman's lawyers about a possible guilty plea, further attempts to get Plumbers' files from the White House, evaluation of national-security claims raised by the defendants, and waiting for the return of the Watergate cover-up indictment.

The decision to develop more facts before the grand jury and to analyze the violations to be charged was made at a meeting with Cox on September 14. This led to our decision to indict Krogh for perjury. Krogh, in fact, was one of the weak links in our proof regarding the break-in. Until his guilty plea and sentencing, Krogh had declined our requests to talk with him informally, and we were not about to take him before the grand jury without knowing what he might say, or the extent of his recollection. We were afraid he would try to protect Ehrlichman from the potentially damaging August 11 memo.

We also felt we did not have sufficient evidence against Colson. There was strong circumstantial evidence that he must have known about the break-in, but there was no direct evidence of such knowledge. In addition, I was strongly convinced that Colson's desire to ruin Ellsberg, destroy his credibility, and try him in the press constituted obstruction of justice in depriving Ellsberg of a fair trial. But here again the evidence was thin, and legal precedents nonexistent. We concluded that further work was needed on Colson's involvement. In this connection, I felt that Hunt knew more than he had testified to, and that he was protecting Colson. After Krogh was sentenced, we questioned him for twelve hours on January 28 and 29.

His apparent inability to remember what he had told Ehrlichman about the Fielding operation was disturbing. I was not certain whether this was the result of conscious or subconscious pressures. Given the closeness between Krogh and Ehrlichman and the strong White House antagonism toward Ellsberg, which everyone testified to, it would have been perfectly natural for Krogh to have told Ehrlichman that Hunt and Liddy were pros, and that they could conduct the break-in so that no one would discover it. All the evidence that I was aware of made me feel certain that Krogh had in fact done just that. However, this closeness to Ehrlichman was also contributing to our problem. Krogh seemed to be trying to protect Ehrlichman from any responsibility for the break-in. In addition, during the interviews in January, Krogh made clear the extent of his concern about Ehrlichman.

He said he was afraid that Ehrlichman might take his own life if he was not able to come to terms with himself by pleading guilty.

But there was another aspect of Krogh's personality that was evident. Krogh felt so guilty about the break-in that he apparently needed to take all the blame for it. This was illustrated by his conduct when we interviewed him in February, after he had started to serve his sentence. He was brought to our office in handcuffs, which were removed by the deputy marshals when the interview began. At lunch time I had other business to attend to, so I suggested he and the marshals go out to eat. To my surprise, Krogh requested that he be handcuffed. His guilt was so great that he actually wanted to be seen in public with handcuffs on.

On January 30, we took Krogh before the grand jury. I kept my questions about what Ehrlichman was told rather vague and unspecific in order to avoid pushing Krogh too far and committing him to testimony that he or we might have trouble with at a later date. His testimony was satisfactory, but it left me with serious reservations as to whether he would ever testify strongly enough concerning Ehrlichman's knowledge. I was even more worried about how he would hold up under cross-examination.

After Krogh's guilty plea, I felt we should devise some way of opening up communications with Ehrlichman in order to explore the possibility of a plea from him. I mentioned this to Jaworski on December 4. We recognized that the primary problem we faced here was the fact that John Wilson, the attorney who represented Ehrlichman in Washington, also represented Haldeman. We were concerned that because of this, Ehrlichman might be influenced by the President through Haldeman.

So on December 5, I suggested to Leon that we write a letter to Wilson inquiring whether his representation of Ehrlichman and Haldeman might constitute a conflict of interest. We would raise the conflict problem in the hope that we could get Joe Ball, Ehrlichman's attorney in the California burglary case, into the picture. It would have been improper for us to have talked to Ball directly, since Wilson was Ehrlichman's attorney in Washington.

Leon agreed and I drafted such a letter, which was mailed on December 10. This resulted in a telephone call from Wilson requesting a meeting to discuss the conflict question. I suggested that Wilson might want to involve Ball in such a meeting because our discussions might relate to the California case. Wilson agreed, and after a few more telephone calls between the three of us, such a meeting was arranged.

During these phone calls, I advised Wilson and Ball of the various charges that Ehrlichman faced: the Fielding break-in, the Watergate cover-up, and perjury. In one of the calls to Ball, I brought up the subject of a plea. Ball replied that they had been thinking about it and wondered if it would be possible to accomplish it in a way that would preserve Ehrlichman's right to practice law. I explained that this had been our rationale for dropping the perjury charges against Krogh after he pled guilty to the break-in. We were on the right track!

On January 10, Leon and I met with Ehrlichman, Wilson, and Ball and discussed Wilson's possible conflict of interest in his continued representation of Ehrlichman and Haldeman. We also discussed all the charges facing Ehrlichman, the possibility that we might be willing to take a plea to less than all the charges, and the fact that this might make it possible for him to practice law some time in the future. Leon stated that we would advise them by letter of the plea we would accept.

The only time Ehrlichman spoke during the meeting, he sounded almost paranoid. He railed against what he described as "selective prosecution." I assumed he meant that the same things had been done by other administrations but had not resulted in any prosecutions.

After the meeting, we began the process of deciding what plea we would accept, and putting our proposal in writing. In the Fielding case, Ehrlichman faced charges of the civil-rights violation for the break-in, which carried a ten-year sentence, and two or three five-year perjury charges. In the Watergate cover-up, he would be charged with obstruction of justice for the cover-up, which was a five-year felony, and perjury. It was my feeling that if we required Ehrlichman to plead guilty to perjury or obstruction of justice, he would recognize that he could probably never expect to practice law again. However, if he pled guilty to the civil-rights violation for the Fielding break-in, he could expect to be suspended from practicing law, but might be reinstated after a few years. So I suggested that we accept a guilty plea to the Fielding break-in alone, and not file any other charges. The charge in the Fielding break-in should be worded in such a way that it would be clear Ehrlichman was involved in the Watergate cover-up in order to cover up the Fielding break-in.

The members of the Watergate cover-up task force were at first violently opposed to this. Gradually, they were persuaded to support my suggestion; however, they proposed that we initially tell Ehrlichman's attorney that we would not accept anything less than two felonies, the Fielding break-in and the Watergate cover-up, and that if Ehrlichman's lawyers turned this down, we then offer what I proposed. A letter setting forth our requirement of a guilty plea to the two felonies was sent to Ehrlichman's attorneys on January 17.

On January 30, Joe Ball called Leon and turned down our written proposal. When Leon responded that we would take a plea to the Fielding break-in that made it clear that Ehrlichman was also involved in the Watergate cover-up in order to prevent the Fielding break-in from being revealed, Ball said he would recommend this to Ehrlichman. The next day Leon phoned Ball, and we read to him the language of the proposed charge.

We had many subsequent telephone calls from one or the other of Ehrlichman's lawyers, in which they requested more time for their client's decision. It seemed clear they were recommending that Ehrlichman accept our last proposal. However, on February 22 we were finally told that Ehrlichman would not plead guilty to any charge. I felt certain that Ehrlichman's decision was the result of pressure by Haldeman and the President.

Our discussions about the type of plea we would accept from Ehrlichman was the source of some disagreement within the Watergate Special Prosecution Force. The friction was not limited to members of the Watergate cover-up task force about whether Ehrlichman should be required to plead to the cover-up. It included a feeling on the part of many younger lawyers on the staff that Leon had made up his mind without giving them an opportunity to participate in the decision.

I had been close enough to the situation and involved enough in the decision to conclude that the critics were mistaken. However, I recognized that Leon operated much differently than Archie. Leon handled matters like the senior partner in a law firm (which he was), and not like a law-school professor (which Archie was). As a result, there seemed to be less give-and-take or openness under Leon than there had been with Archie, although each was equally dedicated to the same end. I suggested to Henry Ruth, and later to Leon, that for the sake of morale, it would be advisable to allow more members of the staff to express their views on controversial matters in the future. Leon leaned over backwards to do this in considering whether or not to indict Nixon.

Our efforts to obtain documents relating to the Plumbers from the White House prior to the indictment were intensified after Archie was fired. Leon sent his second letter requesting Plumber documents on December 5. Two weeks later, after several telephone calls, this led to Chuck Breyer being given access to certain files selected by the White House. This review revealed evidence of removal of some documents and tampering with others. It was perhaps for this reason that Fred Buzhardt, special counsel to the President, initially refused to allow Breyer to retain a copy of the notes he made during his review, or for us to receive copies of the documents that he had reviewed.

As a consequence of this reaction to our request for documents, and in an effort to counteract Nixon's claim that one member of the executive branch could not take another member of the executive branch to court, Leon sent a letter to Senator Eastland, chairman of the Judiciary Committee, on February 14. This letter clearly demonstrated that the White House's claim of cooperation was patently false.

During this period, the White House was receiving its share of criticism from the press. The eighteen-and-a half-minute gap in one of the President's tapes was referred to editorially by the *Washington Post* on January 16 as what it was—"Destruction of Evidence." On January 17, William Buckley's column in the *Washington Star* suggested that Nixon would resign not only with honor, but also with pleasure. The tape erasure moved James Kilpatrick, who had been a strong supporter of the President, to write on January 24 in the *Washington Post* that he had reached the end of his rope in defending the President. Articles regarding impeachment appeared almost daily, and the cartoonists had a field day.

On February 25, Anthony Lewis wrote in the *New York Times:* "There is no respect for the truth. . . . We are infected by corruption at the top."

The constant pressure of the press helped spur us on. Occasionally the White House would seem to seize the initiative, and our morale would sag. The columnists renewed our conviction that what we were doing was right, and that truth and justice would finally prevail.

Our efforts to obtain documents from the White House were always resisted by claims of national security. First with Cox and then with Jaworski, the White House claimed that if the Plumbers task force attempted to get documents, proceeded with our investigation, or returned an indictment, it would damage national security. Initially, we were expected to desist simply because this magic phrase had been invoked. When neither Archie nor Leon were dissuaded by this, Fred Buzhardt or General Alexander Haig, the President's chief of staff, would explain a particular matter affecting national security that they feared would be exposed if we continued. In every case, Cox or Jaworski either felt the matter would not be exposed, or disagreed that such exposure would have any adverse effect on national security. Articles by Seymour Hersch in the *New York Times* also helped expose the fallaciousness of the White House arguments about national security.

I spent several hours listening to Colson's attorney argue about the numerous classified documents he would subpoena for trial if his client were indicted. He contended that the trial judge would rule that he had a right to these documents, but that we would refuse to produce them, with the result that the judge would dismiss the charges against his client. I was convinced this argument would not succeed. I did not believe any of the documents he referred to were legally relevant to, or a justification for, the break-in at Dr. Fielding's office. Judge Gesell's denial of Krogh's attempted national-security defense of the perjury charges was great comfort here.

In addition, I felt we were on strong ground in relying on the Fourth Amendment to the Constitution. Adopted in 1789 as one of the provisions in the Bill of Rights, this amendment states that "The right of the people to be secure in their persons, houses, papers and effects against unreasonable searches and seizures shall not be violated." These words seemed to stand squarely and unequivocally against the action we were challenging.

The right to be secure from unreasonable searches and seizure came to Americans through many years of experience under English Common Law. There, William Pitt once described it movingly as follows: "The poorest Englishman may in his cottage bid defiance to all the force of the Crown. It may be frail, its roof may shake, the wind may blow through it, the storm may enter, the rain may enter. But the King of England may not enter; all his force dare not cross the threshold."

Protection of the Fourth Amendment was a vitally important aspect of our struggle for freedom from Great Britain. In the early Colonial period, agents of the king had the power to enter into any colonist's home or place of business on the merest suspicion of smuggled goods. They had this power under an order of the king called a "writ of assistance."

In 1761, with the death of King George II, the writs automatically expired. The merchants of Boston retained James Otis to petition the Superior Court to prohibit the renewal of these hated writs. John Adams, who was in the courtroom during the argument on Otis's petition, wrote:

> I do say in the most solemn manner that Mr. Otis' oration against the Writs of Assistance breathed into this nation the breath of life. He was a flame of fire; every man of a crowded audience appeared to me to go away as I did, ready to take arms against the Writs of Assistance. Then and there was the first scene of opposition to the arbitrary claims of Great Britain. Then and there the child Independence was born. In fifteen years, namely 1776, he grew to manhood and declared himself free.*

*Nelson B. Lasson, *The History and Development of the Fourth Amendment to the United States Constitution* (New York: AMS Press, 1988), 58–59.

With such a background, it did not seem right to the Watergate Special Prosecution Force that an American citizen should be deprived of this constitutional protection by the mere claim of national security.

As we got closer to reaching a final decision on the charges to be made and the defendants to be included in the Fielding indictment, it became apparent that we would have to wait for the return of the Watergate cover-up indictment because of its possible connection with the President. That indictment was being delayed while the staff considered the question of whether the President should be indicted. It was also delayed until after the Mitchell-Stans jury was selected and sequestered in New York, in order not to prejudice Mitchell in that case.

My first discussion with Jaworski about the President was on December 18. He commented on the possibility of Nixon's resignation and the widespread concern about granting him immunity from prosecution. On January 14, Leon met with the heads of all the task forces to discuss with them how to treat the President, and our obligation to inform the Rodino Committee about the extent of the President's involvement as this appeared from the tapes. Leon solicited views from all members of the staff on how Nixon should be treated. By February 14, it appeared he had decided not to indict the President.

I felt, as several other members of the staff did, that Leon should indict Nixon. Many outside the office felt the same way. Whether any of us would have made the same decision, if we had actually had the responsibility for it, is something about which we can never be certain.

The only remaining question was what the grand jury should say about Nixon, and the manner in which such information should be released. When Ehrlichman's attorneys advised us on February 22 that he would not plead guilty, the return of both indictments was scheduled for the first part of March. The Watergate cover-up indictment was returned on March 1, and the Fielding break-in indictment was returned on March 7.

In the Fielding case, we had previously decided that the break-in should fall under the ten-year-felony civil-rights statute. There were two misdemeanors (one-year maximum jail sentences) that we could have used, but we felt that the break-in was too serious to constitute just a misdemeanor. In reaching our final decision on the defendants, we concluded that there was an overabundance of direct evidence of Ehrlichman's prior knowledge of the break-in. This evidence included apparent perjury by Ehrlichman, in which he denied any review of the Plumbers' files, any advance knowledge of the break-in, and any advance knowledge of a psychological profile on Ellsberg. Four separate counts for such perjury by Ehrlichman were included in the indictment.

By the time our indictment was returned, we felt we had sufficient direct evidence of Colson's participation in a scheme to damage Ellsberg, and enough circumstantial evidence of his knowledge of the break-in, to indict Colson for the break-in. We had abandoned our efforts to charge him with obstruction of justice in interfering with Ellsberg's right to a fair trial, because there were no legal precedents. Also, there was no clear evidence from which we could show that Colson intended to influence Ellsberg's trial jury, which at the time of the break-in had not been selected. In addition, a charge of obstruction of justice could have drawn us more deeply into the web of national security, the defense of Daniel Ellsberg, and the war in Vietnam—all explosive and controversial issues.

The only remaining major decision regarding our indictment was whether we should include Barker, Martinez, and DeDiego as defendants. The first two had received and were serving long sentences for their part in the Watergate break-in. Howard Hunt had told them that their mission in California involved a traitor. But he had also told them that what they were going to do was something that could not be done by the FBI or the CIA, and they admitted to us that they knew if they were caught, they might go to jail. They testified that the name Ellsberg, which they were given only minutes before the break-in, meant nothing to them. They had never heard of Dr. Fielding. After the break-in they returned to the hotel, in which they had registered under fictitious names, and drank champagne in celebration of their successful operation.

It seemed to us that Barker, Martinez, and DeDiego should be held as responsible for the break-in as any of the others. Our decision to indict

Barker and Martinez was not intended to cause them any further imprisonment. In fact, we felt their Watergate sentences were adequate to cover both break-ins, and were willing to so advise the trial judge. We felt, however, it should be made clear that anyone who participated in such activity at any level would be held liable.

We did not submit to the grand jury any question of the President's involvement in the Fielding break-in. Ehrlichman denied telling the President about it until after it occurred, the President had stated he did not know about it until March 1973, and there was no direct evidence sufficient to disprove their statements.

Despite the lack of such evidence, I did not believe Ehrlichman or the President. I felt their relationship was so close, and the President's interest in Ellsberg was so great, that Ehrlichman must have told the President about the break-in prior to its occurrence.

The President's interest in Ellsberg was apparent from listening to the July 24, 1971, tape in which he instructed Krogh to find out all he could about Ellsberg. Nixon also told Krogh to read the chapter on Alger Hiss in his book "Six Crises." Other evidence made it appear that the President was obsessed with Ellsberg. The obsession seemed to begin with Nixon's efforts to prevent the publication of the Pentagon Papers.

Immediately after the Pentagon Papers appeared in the *New York Times* on June 13, 1971, the President directed the Attorney General to obtain a court injunction against further publication. This was done on June 16, and the case went quickly to the Supreme Court. The Court held an unusual Saturday hearing on June 26.

The next day, a staff attorney in the Justice Department was rushed to California to sign the indictment against Ellsberg on Monday, June 28, because the United States attorney in Los Angeles refused to sign it. Such a move could only have been done with the knowledge and approval of the President, and seemed calculated to influence the Supreme Court in its consideration of the Pentagon Papers case. The Supreme Court, however, quashed the injunction on June 30 and allowed the continued publication of the Pentagon Papers.

In his concurring opinion, Justice Black described the responsibility of a free press to expose governmental deception, in words that were equally appropriate to Watergate:

> Only a free and unrestrained press can effectively expose deception in government. And paramount among the responsibilities of a free press is the duty to prevent any part of the Government from deceiving the people and sending them off to distant lands to die of foreign fevers and foreign shot and shell. In my view, far from deserving condemnation for their courageous reporting, *The New York Times, The Washington Post* and other newspapers should be commended for serving the purpose that the Founding Fathers saw so clearly. In revealing the workings of government that led to the Vietnam war, the newspapers nobly did precisely that which the founders hoped and trusted they would do.

In the beginning of July, the President received a memo from Colson that proposed that the theft and publication of the Pentagon Papers could be used to Nixon's advantage in the presidential election in 1972, if he could tie Ellsberg and his radical friends to the Democrats. Colson's memo concluded by warning that in order for such a scheme to be successful, Ellsberg would have to be convicted. The President's efforts in this regard were revealed later by Colson when he identified the President as the person who had made the request that something be gotten out on Ellsberg, which resulted in the release of Bunt's vile memo about Ellsberg's attorney in August 1971. Nixon's obsession with Ellsberg and having him convicted also seemed apparent in the offer of the directorship of the FBI to Judge Byrne and in the President's reluctance to allow the fact of the break-in to be reported to the judge. Also, there was Young's testimony that when he talked with Ehrlichman about the August 11 break-in memo in April, 1971, he stated to Ehrlichman that he assumed Ehrlichman had cleared it with higher authority—to which Ehrlichman replied, "That is a question you should not ask."

So although there was no direct evidence that the President had advance knowledge about the Fielding break-in, I felt certain he did. However, there was no point in pursuing it in view of the clear evidence of his knowledge of, and participation in, the Watergate cover-up.

10

Preparing for Trial

This case involves the issue of whether security is to be made more important than liberty and freedom, and particularly, security as defined by one person who claims he is immune from the restraints of the law.

—*from the trial notes of William H. Merrill*

Although all our efforts from the beginning of the investigation were in preparation for a trial, they took on a new and greater significance after the indictment was returned. The first problem was whether there would ever be a trial to prepare for. When the Watergate cover-up indictment was returned on March 1, Judge Sirica indicated he wanted that case to come to trial first. Some of the members of my task force suggested privately that Sirica, having been named *Time's* Man of the Year for 1973, was trying for two in a row. We were afraid that if the cover-up case was tried before our break-in case, the Special Prosecutor might decide not to take the break-in case to trial, because it would look like we were harassing Ehrlichman and Colson, who were defendants in both cases. We did not think there would be the same problem if our case came to trial first, because there was so much more public interest in the cover-up case.

So on March 4, I began discussions in the office to explore how we could persuade Sirica to assign our case to another judge. We preferred Judge

Gesell because of his previous familiarity with the case through Krogh's indictment for perjury and subsequent guilty plea to the break-in. The next day there was a newspaper story that the other judges of the district court were unhappy with Sirica's attempts to retain control over all Watergate cases, so I discussed my suggestion further with Leon. He agreed to mention it to Judge Sirica. My efforts were successful on March 8, when Sirica assigned our case to Gesell.

When Judge Sirica set September 1 for the trial of the cover-up case, at the arraignment on March 9, we then had to position our case with Judge Gesell so that it could be over far enough in advance of September 1 to allow Ehrlichman and Colson sufficient time to prepare for the cover-up trial. Otherwise, there might not be any trial of our case.

We received some help in this from Judge Gesell. The possibility of having the break-in trial first occurred to him also, and on March 11, he telephoned me and asked my views on the order of the trials. I replied that I would have to discuss that with Jaworski. I added that our case might take only two weeks to try, unless we encountered problems with the defendants' national-security claims. He seemed quite surprised at my prediction of the length of the trial. I discussed Judge Gesell's inquiry with Leon, and we agreed we should not make any recommendation as to the order of the trials; we would just let events take their natural course. On April 11, Judge Gesell set June 17 for the trial of the Fielding break-in case.

Another immediate problem was the continued pressure regarding a trial of the California burglary case. On March 1, I called the Los Angeles district attorney and suggested a meeting in Washington right after our indictment was returned, to discuss the dismissal of their case. On March 11 we met, and they agreed to drop the burglary case. They kept open the perjury charges they had against Ehrlichman, so we were still concerned about an early trial in California on Ehrlichman's perjury charges. On April 2, that worry was removed when the Los Angeles district attorney obtained an adjournment of Ehrlichman's perjury case.

My statement to Judge Gesell regarding the length of our trial was based on discussions that my trial team had already begun in an effort to narrow the issues before the jury to just the break-in itself and those responsible for it. From the beginning of the investigation, we had recognized the necessity of avoiding what might appear to be a defense of Daniel Ellsberg, or a justification of his involvement in the release of the Pentagon Papers. For this reason, I did not contact Ellsberg until after the indictment was returned. Thereafter, I felt we should interview Ellsberg in order to learn whether he had any information that we should be aware of prior to the trial.

Prior to meeting Ellsberg, I had been in favor of the release of the Pentagon Papers and ending the war in Vietnam. I recognized that these feelings might affect my judgment about Ellsberg; nevertheless, I was impressed by Ellsberg's intensity and sincerity. By any standard, one would have to admit that Ellsberg certainly had affected history by his release of the Pentagon Papers.

In becoming one of the chief spokesmen for the antiwar sentiment in the country, he also became the chief target of the Nixon White House. Nixon perceived Ellsberg as a dangerous obstacle to his plans for ending the war. In large part, Ellsberg's activities and Nixon's obsession with Ellsberg eventually led to the impeachment hearings and forced the President's resignation. If the break-in at Dr. Fielding's office in September 1971 had not taken place, the break-in at the Democratic National Headquarters in June 1972 at the Watergate, by the same individuals, might never have taken place, and the President would have finished his term in office.

From our meeting with Ellsberg, the ultimate purpose of the break-in became clearer. The release of derogatory information about Ellsberg, and the public discrediting of him, was not just an end in itself. The President also wanted to stop Ellsberg from talking about the war in Vietnam. More specifically, Nixon was afraid Ellsberg knew of Nixon's and Kissinger's belief that they could threaten the North Vietnamese sufficiently so they would agree to withdraw from South Vietnam as part of the settlement of the war. Nixon was prepared to go to any lengths to force the North Vietnamese to accept such a settlement, and had a "game plan" for escalating our activities in Vietnam in order to implement his threats and bring about North Vietnam's acquiescence. The President was afraid Ellsberg knew of the plan of escalation and would reveal it publicly. He was concerned that such a revelation would cause increased opposition to the war and make it impossible for him to end it on his terms. This, he felt, would adversely affect his image as a strong President. From the President's point of view, the discrediting of Ellsberg (including his conviction of the charges he faced) would either frighten Ellsberg into silence, or would make anything he said so unbelievable that it would not interfere with Nixon's plans. Although none of this would be useful in the trial of our case, I suggested that Ellsberg speak with John Doar, counsel for the House Impeachment Committee.

Our additional efforts to narrow the issues for the jury related to reducing the numbers of witnesses we would use by eliminating those who had only an indirect connection with our case or who might open up unrelated areas that could be troublesome. Henry Kissinger appeared to have some knowledge of the Plumbers' operations but not of the break-in, and if we called him, it would involve us in such a morass of national security that the trial could go on for months and the break-in be forgotten. So we eliminated Kissinger as our witness. Daniel Ellsberg was clearly an interested party in the break-in, but his presence would have also involved us in the national-security trap and we decided not to use him. John Dean could have provided some helpful testimony in proving one of the perjury charges against Ehrlichman. But the question of Dean's credibility had received such intense publicity that we wanted to avoid having it become an issue in our case, so we did not call him. Several CIA employees could have been called as witnesses to the preparation of the psychological profile on Ellsberg (which Young and Krogh referred to in the August 11 break-in memo), but this was not necessary to our case and might again have drawn us into arguments about national security, so we did not use them.

Our major concern about witnesses was still how strong Krogh and Young would be in describing what they told Ehrlichman about the "covert operation." Young seemed to be the weakest, and at times I wondered if he was protecting Henry Kissinger, his former boss. I had the feeling

Young believed the safety of the country would be seriously undermined if Kissinger's position as secretary of state was threatened. This was not just because of Kissinger's admitted capability in foreign affairs, but primarily because of Nixon's decreased capacity to be involved in carrying out his presidential responsibilities and his lack of credibility due to Watergate. Similar opinions were expressed by others in the press. Yet on one occasion, after Kissinger testified before the Senate Foreign Relations Committee that he had no knowledge of the Plumbers' activities, Young suggested that this answer should be read very carefully. He said, "Maybe Henry didn't know anything about the Plumbers because he was not aware of that name, but he sure knew what David Young was doing."

With Krogh, the effect of prison caused an unexpected problem. I talked with Krogh at the end of May in preparation for the June 17 trial date. It was the first time I had seen him since just after he had begun to serve his sentence in early February. He seemed more subdued than at our last meeting. I was shocked when early in our session, he said something to the effect that he probably had not said anything to Ehrlichman about the Hunt/ Liddy project prior to the August 11 memo. Until then, he had had difficulty remembering exactly what he had said to Ehrlichman, but he had never stated that he might not have said anything. All I could think of was that as a result of being in that environment for the last sixteen weeks, he had been affected by the prison psychology of not squealing on anyone. Deciding to take a calculated risk, I slammed my hand on the desk and shouted, "God dammit, Bud, that's the first time you ever said anything like that. Is that what you have learned from your fellow prisoners? If that is how you intend to implement what you said in court about being sorry for what happened to Dr. Fielding, then you can go to hell. I won't interview you any further. I'll call you as an adverse witness and cross-examine your ass off!"—and I strode out of the room, hoping I had not gone too far.

My shock treatment worked. Krogh's conscience was stronger than his pride and we were able to continue as openly as previously, after his attorney tactfully suggested we had misunderstood each other. The final straw with Krogh seemed to come on June 6, when I reviewed with him the areas of

Ehrlichman's perjury. The fact that Ehrlichman was lying about some related matters helped Krogh admit to himself that Ehrlichman must have known about the break-in. He also recognized that Ehrlichman was lying to avoid any responsibility for the break-in and was trying to put the entire blame on Krogh and Young. Krogh no longer felt the need for self-flagellation, and this knowledge of Ehrlichman's lying seemed to remove the pressure he had felt to protect his former boss.

But Krogh and Young still bothered me, and I was afraid we might be criticized if the jury acquitted Ehrlichman because of their weak testimony. I felt we might be criticized not only for losing but also for bringing the case on such feeble testimony. I wondered if there could be some way of aiding their memories, and of helping us be more certain of whether their poor memories were the result of conscious or subconscious pressures. It occurred to me that we should explore whether the use of sodium pentathol or hypnosis could be helpful. Then no one could accuse us of not doing everything possible to get at the truth.

I discussed my thoughts with Leon. He mentioned the use of sodium pentathol on German prisoners in World War II and approved my exploring this further. Next, I talked with a trial attorney in the Department of Justice who had been involved with the use of hypnosis to enable witnesses of a shooting to remember the license number of a murder car. I then met with two psychiatrists and discussed these methods further. Ultimately, I concluded that the use of drugs or hypnosis could boomerang and subject us to severe criticism. We would, of course, do nothing without Krogh's or Young's approval, make a complete audio and visual record of everything we did, and provide a complete disclosure to the defendants and the jury. However, at best it could raise serious questions as to whether the witness's testimony was his real recollection or one that had been artificially induced. At worst, it might appear that we had adopted the methods of a police state—the very concept and methods we were opposing.

Shortly before the trial, we took one final step because of our concern about Krogh and Young. We filed a motion requesting the judge to call Krogh, Young, and Hunt as the Court's witnesses. We argued that because of their involvement in the break-in, we did not want to have to vouch for their credibility to the jury. Additionally, this would have given us the right to cross-examine them, something an attorney can not generally do with his own witness. However, Judge Gesell denied our motion, so we were left with our concerns about how they would finally testify.

I went through somewhat the same considerations in determining whether we should hire a team of psychiatrists and sociologists to make a sophisticated evaluation of the prospective jurors, and the type of juror, we should have for our case. Here again, I decided that this was not the type of conduct the Government should engage in. I felt that after eliminating the fairly obvious prejudices and biases, the Government ought to be willing to rest its case with the first twelve jurors in the jury box.

This decision came as somewhat of a surprise to the defense counsel, who during a pretrial hearing before Judge Gesell asked for the results of any jury analysis made by the Special Prosecutor (which they would have been entitled to). When I replied that we had made no such study, Judge Gesell, picking up some objection the defense had made earlier, said, "Now that doesn't sound like a blood-thirsty prosecutor, does it?" I heard Ehrlichman's attorney mutter under his breath as he sat down, "He's a wolf in sheep's clothing."

Another pretrial matter involved the division of witnesses at the trial between me and the other two members of the trial team. In their youthful enthusiasm, my two assistants felt we should divide the trial—opening statement, our witnesses, cross-examination of the defense witnesses, and closing arguments—equally. Although I felt they were competent enough to have done the job on their own, I was concerned whether their trial experience was sufficient to enable them to react adequately to the pressures that would occur in this case. Since I was responsible for the outcome in a way they were not, I decided upon a much different division of the trial, one in which I played a far greater role.

My decision was also influenced by my conviction that in any jury trial, particularly a criminal case, where there are multiple attorneys on one side, the jury has to be able to look to one attorney as the spokesman for that side.

The jury must be able to feel an identification with one attorney, and this essential relationship cannot be developed if the trial is fragmented between different attorneys for the same side.

In our case, this would be particularly important in the cross-examination of Ehrlichman. I had to be the one who cross-examined him, and it would have to be me against Ehrlichman in the minds of the jury. So I would have to give the opening and closing arguments in order that I could talk about the evidence that I had elicited from Ehrlichman.

In addition, I was conscious that we should try to lessen the appearance that the Government attorneys outnumbered the defense attorneys, and the sympathy the jurors might feel for the defendants because of this.

I was more certain of the correctness of my decision about the division of the trial, and the need for it, when on April 28, John Mitchell and Maurice Stans were acquitted by a jury in New York of charges relating to impeding a Securities and Exchange Commission investigation of Robert Vesco. This acquittal also added new pressures to our trial. The pressure mounted as the Rodino Committee, created in February, became more active and began public hearings on May 10. The outcome of our case would obviously have an effect on the committee's consideration of charges relating to the impeachment of the President.

The other major problem in preparing for trial was contending with the defendants' motions to dismiss our case because of national security and for discovery and production of documents relating to national security. Colson's attorney submitted drafts of such motions to Judge Gesell after the indictment was returned. In preparing our reply, I suggested that we refer to our belief that there was no evidence the President had authorized the break-in. My associates were concerned that this would raise a question over the extent of the President's power and involve us in a debate over the merits of the national-security defense. On the contrary, I thought it was the best argument for avoiding such a debate. My position prevailed, and this part of our response persuaded Judge Gesell to require the defendants to file affidavits to support their claims that they had been acting with presidential authorization. They were unable to do so.

Phil Heyman had returned during the summer recess at Harvard Law School to help us in preparing for trial. He was also eager to argue the national-security motion. I knew his scholarly approach would impress Judge Gesell, so I agreed to let him argue that motion.

Judge Gesell held hearings for four days at the end of May on the defendants' national-security motions and other pretrial matters. The day after the last motion was argued, the judge denied the motions to dismiss the case because of national security and because of pretrial publicity.

In the judge's opinion, reported in volume 376 of Federal Supplement at page 29, he said:

Defendants contend that even though the Fourth Amendment would ordinarily prohibit break-ins of this nature, the President had the authority, by reason of his special responsibilities over foreign relations and national defense, to suspend its requirements and that he did so in this case. Neither assertion is accurate. Many of the landmark Fourth Amendment cases in this country and in England concerned citizens accused of disloyal or treasonous conduct, for history teaches that such suspicions foster attitudes within a government that generate conduct inimical to individual rights. . . . The judicial response to such Executive overreaching has been consistent and emphatic: the Government must comply with the strict constitutional and statutory limitations on trespassory searches and arrests even when known foreign agents are involved. . . . To hold otherwise, except under the most exigent circumstances, would be to abandon the Fourth Amendment to the whim of the Executive in total disregard of the Amendment's history and purpose.

The Fourth Amendment protects the privacy of citizens against unreasonable and unrestrained intrusion by Government officials and their agents. It is not theoretical. It lies at the heart of our free society. As the Supreme Court recently remarked, "no right is held more sacred." . . .

The security of one's privacy against arbitrary intrusion by governmental authorities has proven essential to our concept of ordered liberty. . . . No right so fundamental should now, after the long struggle

against governmental trespass, be diluted to accommodate conduct of
the very type the Fourth Amendment was designed to outlaw.

The opinion relied heavily on the President's public denial of any prior
knowledge of the break-in, and on the defendants' failure to contradict this
denial. Despite the legal basis for his ruling, Judge Gesell indicated that the
defendants would be allowed to advise the jury fully as to why they did what
they did, and that they were entitled to the production of documents that
were necessary for them to do this.

The other important pretrial motion concerned whether there had been
so much publicity that the defendants could not receive a fair trial. There
had been probably more publicity relating to Watergate than regarding any
previous case. However, the amount of publicity was not the determining
factor. The crucial question was whether the publicity had prejudiced the
jurors against the defendants.

We respected the presumption of innocence that each defendant was
entitled to, and were equally concerned that they receive a fair trial; but
we did not feel anyone could accurately assess the effect of the publicity, or
whether it was prejudicial, until the prospective jurors were selected and
questioned at the beginning of the trial. We felt that only then could Judge
Gesell determine whether we could have jurors with open minds, who had
not prejudged the case and who would decide the guilt or innocence of each
defendant solely on the evidence presented in court. So we suggested that a
ruling on this motion be deferred until an effort had been made to select a
jury. Judge Gesell agreed with us.

Closely allied with this was whether the defendants could receive a fair
trial in Washington, D.C., because there might have been more Watergate
publicity in Washington than elsewhere. The defendants said they were
willing to go anywhere. We opposed this because we felt the Watergate publicity was nationwide. Besides, we argued, moving the trial to an area where
there might be less publicity than in Washington would be self-defeating
because the announcement of such a move and the arrival of reporters to
cover the trial would cause a deluge of publicity in the location selected.
Judge Gesell agreed with our position on this also.

During the hearings on the motions, it was apparent that Ehrlichman would be represented by four attorneys, two from Miami and two from the District of Columbia. The two Washington lawyers were black and had obviously been retained by Ehrlichman in an effort to influence the trial jury, which he anticipated would be largely black. I wondered if the attorneys knew they were being used, and hoped the jurors would see through this move and resent it.

In announcing his ruling on the motions, Judge Gesell also criticized the President for failing to comply with the defendants' subpoenas for documents, and for a while it sounded as though he might hold Nixon in contempt. This refusal by the President to comply with the defendants' subpoenas almost blew our case out of the water. On May 30, I suggested to Jaworski that we should support the judge by filing a brief in which we agreed with the defendants' arguments regarding their right to see documents in the White House. Although I recognized that in doing this, there was a chance that our case might be dismissed, I could not believe the President would risk the adverse effects of preventing the case from being tried. I took some comfort from several articles in the press at this time that suggested any such action by Nixon would be grounds for impeachment.

On June 3, we avoided a direct confrontation with the White House by suggesting to Judge Gesell that the defendants' subpoenas were too broad and did not refer to specific documents. The judge agreed, and the subpoenas were rewritten. However, the problem remained when the President still refused to comply with Ehrlichman's subpoena. As a result, on June 11, Gesell severed the trial of Ehrlichman from the other defendants' and ordered the trial of the others to begin a week later.

We certainly did not want to try Ehrlichman alone, nor did we want to try Liddy, Barker, and Martinez without Ehrlichman. After much thought, we decided we could avoid this problem if Fred Buzhardt had reviewed the White House files and found nothing covered by Ehrlichman's subpoena, and would sign an affidavit to that effect. Buzhardt confirmed this and agreed to sign such an affidavit. At a hearing the next day, we presented Buzhardt's affidavit to the Court. As a result of this, Judge Gesell reinstated Ehrlichman's case.

That night, Buzhardt suffered a massive heart attack. I felt sorry for him, because I assumed the seizure was brought on by having faced an angry Nixon on his return from court. On June 14, the judge set June 26 as the final date for the trial of all the defendants. During our jousting over the wording of the document subpoenas, Ehrlichman indicated that he also intended to subpoena the President as a witness.

Judge Gesell stated that he would not enforce such a subpoena and suggested that Ehrlichman explore the possibility of serving written interrogatories on the President. Thereafter, Ehrlichman's counsel presented us with a long, detailed set of interrogatories. We objected to them because we felt they were merely another device to cause an adjournment, a mistrial, or a reversal on appeal, since they called for answers that involved matters of national security or executive privilege, which the President would obviously not give.

Judge Gesell agreed that the interrogatories were improper and said they would not be authorized. He did the same to a revised set. Finally, over our objection, he approved six questions to the President.

In attempting to comply with the subpoenas for documents relating to national security, we were confronted with another problem. When the indictment was drafted, we felt we might be broadening the basis for the admissibility of evidence by alleging that one of the purposes of the conspiracy was to conceal the fact of the break-in. Although there was considerable evidence of concealment, this part of the indictment enabled Ehrlichman to claim that national security was the reason that the break-in was concealed. The problem became intensified during Judge Gesell's attempts to force the President to allow Ehrlichman to have access to his own notes in the White House files—which the President refused to do. We rescued the situation by stating that we would not offer any evidence in support of the concealment allegations.

In the final days of our preparation for trial, we were involved in discussions with counsel for Barker and Martinez over possible guilty pleas by them, but at the last minute they decided against this. Judge Gesell had previously dismissed the charges against DeDiego because the judge felt that some testimony DeDiego had given to a grand jury in Miami, before the Special Prosecutor was appointed, resulted in DeDiego having immunity from prosecution.

During this period, my life consisted entirely in preparing for the trial, pausing occasionally for eating and sleeping. The latter was interrupted one night when I got up at 4:00 A.M. to drive to the nearest gas station that had gas. My gas tank was almost empty, and I had had difficulty finding a station that had gas. I waited for two hours for the station to open, and another hour until I got up to the pump. During the wait, I wondered whether Nixon's preoccupation with Watergate and his apparent lack of leadership had encouraged the Arab world to make this problem worse than it otherwise might have been.

The June 2 issue of the *Washington Post* contained a review of *All the President's Men,* and a cartoon by Maxwell Silverstein depicting all the characters in the Fielding break-in, entitled "The National Security Streak-in."

During the final days of preparation for trial, we received some assistance from an unexpected source—Charles Colson's conscience.

11

Colson Pleads Guilty

As Justice Davis said over 100 years ago: "The Constitution of the United States is a law for rulers and people, equally in war and in peace, and covers with the shield of its protection all classes of men at all times under all circumstances. No doctrine involving more pernicious consequences was ever invented by the wit of man than that any of its provisions can be suspended during any of the great exigencies of government. Such a doctrine leads directly to anarchy or despotism, but the theory of necessity on which it is based is false, for the Government, within the Constitution, has all the powers granted to it which are necessary to preserve its existence, as has been happily proved by the result of the great effort to throw off its authority."

—Justice David Davis, 1866 as quoted in
the trial notes of William H. Merrill

O f all the President's aides, Colson had the reputation of being the most unprincipled. During the 1968 presidential campaign, he was quoted as saying he would walk over his grandmother to reelect Nixon. From the beginning of the publicity about Watergate, Colson was mentioned as being the architect of the cover-up, and perhaps even the break-in. In addition to his efforts to discredit Ellsberg and his apparent involvement in the Fielding break-in, there was evidence that he had sent Hunt to Chappaquiddick to get something derogatory on Senator Edward Kennedy, that he had Hunt forge a cable to make it appear that President

Kennedy had been involved in the assassination of Ziem in Vietnam, that he had organized an attempt by Hunt's Cuban American friends to beat up Ellsberg on the Capitol steps during an antiwar protest, and that he had suggested the firebombing of Brookings Institute because its executives were suspected of leaking classified information to the press.

The possibility of Colson's involvement in such activities was almost constantly in the press after the Watergate break-in in July 1972. It was this unfavorable publicity that finally led to his guilty plea in June 1974.

It may seem strange that it took so long for Colson's conscience to persuade him to plead guilty, but it was probably a natural result of the atmosphere that existed in the Nixon White House. At a meeting of Colson's staff in July 1971, during a discussion of his memo to the President regarding tying Ellsberg to the Democrats in order to assist in Nixon's reelection, only one member of the staff questioned the ethics of Colson's comment that this plan would require the conviction of Ellsberg. A young White House Fellow, who was at that time a law student, objected to the propriety of doing anything that would adversely affect Ellsberg, in view of the fact that he was under indictment and facing trial. The objection was brushed aside, and the meeting went on to consider how great it would be to "get" Ellsberg. What agonies the nation would have been spared if this objection had been considered more thoroughly at the time, rather than after the damage had been done.

Jaworski and I met with Colson and David Shapiro, his attorney, on December 7 to listen to their arguments that Colson should not be indicted as one of the conspirators in the Fielding break-in. They said he did not know about it in advance. We were not persuaded; the evidence seemed too strong against him. I was surprised by what I thought were tears in Colson's eyes. I was not certain whether this was a sign of remorse for what he had done, or because of our apparent decision to name him as one of the defendants.

I had another meeting with Colson and Shapiro on January 15. For three hours, Colson answered our questions. It was hard to believe he was not telling the truth, but there was too much evidence that seemed to contradict his protestations of innocence. As a result, I wondered if a lie-detector test might help.

I did not want to suggest it directly, because Colson's attorney might use it against me in the future. I wanted it to seem like it was Colson's idea. So I threw the bait to Shapiro by saying, "I can't accept your statement that Chuck is telling me the truth. If you're so certain of it, then you'll have to think of some other way of trying to convince me." He replied, "Give me a few days to decide how to convince you."

I was certain Shapiro would use those "few days" to arrange for a polygraph test. A week later, he presented me with the results of such a test.

From previous experience with polygraphs as an assistant United States attorney, I was skeptical of any test arranged for by a defendant's lawyer. I felt the manner in which the questions were asked and the wording of the questions were important and could affect the accuracy or meaningfulness of the results. I was also aware of situations where the defendant had become so convinced that what he had done was not wrong (tax fraud to cover medical payments for a wife dying of cancer) that he gave no physical responses to the key questions.

In the test given to me by Colson's attorney, one of the questions was "Were you involved in the break-in at Dr. Fielding's office?" This was ambiguous, and the answer therefore meaningless. The word "involved" could be interpreted to mean physically part of, instead of just aware of, and could therefore be answered in the negative by one who was not at the scene but knew about the operation in advance. Even the use of the word "break-in" posed a problem, because it was not planned as a break-in. There were no questions in the test Colson took that explored whether he was "aware someone was going to examine Ellsberg's records in Dr. Fielding's office without the doctor's knowledge or consent."

So I wanted an evaluation of Colson's test by an FBI polygraph expert. Then I would ask if Colson would consent to being questioned by such an expert. After a few days, an FBI examiner said he felt the results of Colson's test were inconclusive. I advised Shapiro of this and asked if Colson would take another test by the Bureau. He declined. Colson's refusal to take such a test was one of the many factors we took into consideration in charging him with being one of the members of the conspiracy to break into Dr. Fielding's office.

Early in the evening on May 23, the last day of the hearings before Judge Gesell on the defendant's motions regarding national security, pretrial publicity, and other matters, I received a phone call from Shapiro at my apartment. He said that Colson was interested in pleading guilty, and that he hoped I would make it possible for him to give his client some good news because his client was very upset. I suspected that Shapiro and Colson must have concluded from Judge Gesell's statements during the arguments over the last four days that the judge was going to deny the motions, and that our evidence was sufficient to convict Colson of the break-in. I also thought Shapiro was hoping we would accept a plea to a misdemeanor, which we had previously turned down. I replied rather shortly, "I can't give you any good news. You know we have always insisted on a plea to the felony charge, and we won't change on this."

Shapiro replied, "No, I mean would you accept a guilty plea to obstruction of justice regarding Ellsberg's right to a fair trial? Because of all the adverse publicity he has faced, Chuck now realizes what Ellsberg must have gone through and it bothers him. He has felt guilty about it for a long time."

I had to restrain myself from going right through the phone and shouting, "You're damn right we'll accept such a plea." We had all but abandoned any chance of making such a charge, and I was disappointed in this because I felt it involved a principle almost as important as that involved in the break-in. I repressed my enthusiasm and said he could tell Chuck we would be interested, but I would have to take it up with Leon, and the cover-up task force would have to be consulted. Colson was also a defendant in the cover-up case, and I realized he would expect those charges to be dropped if he pleaded guilty to obstruction of justice.

During the next few days, we were involved in an evaluation of the effect of Colson's proposed plea. In our case, it would mean the almost certain conviction of Ehrlichman, provided I did an adequate job of cross-examining him. It would confirm our contention that the reason for the break-in was to obtain information against Ellsberg and make it more difficult for Ehrlichman to argue that it involved national security. It would also leave

Ehrlichman all alone, as the only person who would testify that he thought the "covert operation" would be carried out in a manner that did not violate the law.

There was less certainty about the effect of a plea by Colson on the cover-up case because it was not known what, if any, positive testimony Colson would give. Some members of that task force did not trust him.

In one of my discussions with Shapiro, he asked if we would make any recommendation to the judge regarding Colson's sentence. I said we would not.

After a few days, Shapiro wanted to advise Judge Gesell of the possibility that Colson might plead guilty. I felt he hoped to get some reaction from the judge regarding sentence. A discussion with the judge was difficult because he was vacationing on an island off the coast of Maine. Shapiro asked me to call to see if we could come to Maine to discuss the matter personally. When I did, Judge Gesell said the logistics would be too difficult since he would want a court reporter present. He suggested that Shapiro and I phone him from our office and make some arrangement for recording the conversation.

I discovered that the phone originally installed for Archie had a device by which we could record conversations. Although it had never been used by Archie or Leon, I asked my associates to set it up and we made the call on May 28. Shapiro was told we were recording the phone call. During the fifteen-minute conversation, Judge Gesell was careful not to commit himself as to what the sentence would be. When we hung up, I learned that immediately after the call had been placed, an incoming call had been taken on a second line on the phone at Leon's secretary's desk. The effect of this was to disconnect the recording device—and not one word of our conversation was recorded. I dictated a memo about the contents of the call and got Shapiro to approve it.

We had our final bargaining session with Shapiro on May 31. I recall thinking that the younger lawyers wanted to push too hard, and that they felt the older lawyers did not push hard enough. There was probably some truth to both positions, and it made an effective combination. In this case, we got what we wanted, and on June 3, Colson pled guilty to the charge of obstruction of justice. At the time the judge accepted his plea, Colson said:

> I would like this Court to know that I am guilty of the crime charged. Your Honor's words from the bench during the pre-trial hearings two weeks ago, that if this is to be a government of laws and not of men, then those men entrusted with enforcing the law, whatever their motives, must be held to have intended the natural and probable consequence of their acts, had a profound effect on me.
>
> My motive and my purpose in seeking to disseminate derogatory and adverse information about Dr. Ellsberg and his lawyer was to neutralize Dr. Ellsberg as an anti-war spokesman in order to further the President's aims for ending the war in Vietnam. It did not matter to me that Dr. Ellsberg was facing serious criminal charges. It did not matter to me that the statements and information I was seeking to communicate to the public through the press, through other channels such as congressional hearings, could impede, influence or obstruct Dr. Ellsberg's trial.
>
> I now realize that it could have and did have that effect. It was this attitude, your Honor, of not caring, this callousness to the rights of a defendant under a criminal indictment that gave rise to the crime to which I am now pleading.
>
> In the last two years I have become acutely aware of something I was very insensitive to before. I now know what it is like to be a defendant in a celebrated criminal case. Among other things, this experience has taught me to care very much about the rights of criminal defendants and understand how those rights can be jeopardized.
>
> I have come to believe in the very depths of my soul and my being that official threats to those rights such as those charged in this information must be stopped; and by this plea, your Honor, I am prepared to take whatever consequence I must to help in stopping it.

Colson's plea led to some cartoons that played sarcastically on Colson's publicized conversion to Christ.

On June 20, Colson and Krogh were in the office for pretrial interviews. They joked nervously about the fact that the next day, Krogh was to be released from prison, and Colson was to be sentenced and probably would be sent to prison. Judge Gesell sentenced Colson to jail for one to three years. Although Colson and Shapiro seemed shocked, I felt they had been unrealistic if they had not anticipated a jail sentence.

Just prior to his sentence, Colson stated that in acting against Ellsberg, he was doing so on instructions of the President. This led to a further cartoon recalling what Colson had said about walking over his grandmother to reelect Nixon.

12

The Trial

They say this is national security—God save this nation from such security.

—from the trial notes of William H. Merrill

Selecting the Jury

The trial started on Wednesday, June 26, with the selection of the jury. Throughout our investigation, we wondered about the effect of the constant publicity about Watergate and related matters. The defendants had filed motions to change the site of the trial or to adjourn or dismiss the case because of this publicity. We had argued that Judge Gesell should defer any ruling on these motions until an attempt had been made to select the jury.

We wanted to preserve the defendants' rights to a fair trial by an impartial jury. To do otherwise would fly in the face of the very principles we were struggling to protect. The volume of the pretrial publicity was admittedly massive, but no one could predict in advance whether the amount or the content had so affected the potential jurors that we could not obtain an impartial jury. Under the law, it was not necessary to have jurors who had not heard or read of the Fielding break-in. In the case of *Irvin v. Dowd,* the Supreme Court had ruled in 1961 that the vital question was whether as a result of such publicity the potential juror had formed an opinion as to the guilt or innocence of one or more of the defendants, and if so, whether such a juror could lay aside such opinion and render a verdict based on the evidence presented in court. The Court had said:

> It is not required, however, that jurors be totally ignorant of the facts and issues involved. In these days of swift, widespread and diverse methods of communication, an important case can be expected to arouse the interest of the public in the vicinity, and scarcely any of those best qualified to serve as jurors will not have formed some impression or opinion as to the merits of the case. This is particularly true in criminal cases. To hold that the mere existence of any preconceived notion as to the guilt or innocence of an accused, without more evidence, is sufficient to rebut the presumption of a prospective juror's impartiality would be to establish an impossible standard. It is sufficient if the juror can lay aside his impression or opinion and render a verdict based on the evidence presented in Court.

We needed only twelve impartial jurors. However, we recognized that if a large percentage of jurors had to be excused because they believed the defendants were guilty, Judge Gesell or an appellate court might reasonably conclude that a fair trial of this case at that time was impossible. So whether a trial would be held at all, and whether an appellate court would later rule that the trial was fair, depended upon the extent of Judge Gesell's questioning and the answers he received from the prospective jurors.

Prior to the trial, Judge Gesell had requested that all counsel submit a list of questions they wanted him to ask of the prospective jurors. As each panel of thirty prospective jurors was called into the courtroom, the judge described the general nature of the case and asked the entire group questions designed to reveal the most obvious grounds for excusing a juror. Judge Gesell then cleared the courtroom of prospective jurors and spectators. Each prospective juror was called back and questioned by the judge in great detail about the juror's knowledge of the case and his or her ability to decide the guilt or innocence of each defendant on the evidence presented in court.

Occasionally, the judge allowed counsel for defendants to ask additional questions. If an answer raised any reasonable concern about the juror's ability to be impartial, the juror was excused by Judge Gesell, or the judge granted the defendants' request that the juror be excused for cause.

In addition to excusing potential jurors for cause, the Government and each defendant had, as in all cases, the right to excuse a certain number of prospective jurors for other intangible reasons. This is done by what are called "preemptory challenges." We were concerned about having jurors who might be influenced favorably toward the defendants because of a dislike of Ellsberg, or because of being overly impressed with classified documents or national security. We were interested in getting people on the jury who we felt would be receptive to our argument that the break-in was a serious threat to our constitutional rights. We also tried to get young people on the jury, feeling that they might be less inflexible in their attitudes, and that they might be more concerned about governmental abuse and not misled by claims of national security.

Other than these considerations, we simply listened to and observed the reactions of the prospective jurors as they were being questioned by Judge Gesell. My two colleagues and I made a collective evaluation of each juror as the questioning proceeded.

I was impressed by the forthright manner in which the prospective jurors answered Judge Gesell's questions. As a result of the questioning, only 13 of the 120 indicated any unfavorable opinion of the defendants. From this, I felt reassured that the defendants would receive a fair trial.

At the end of two days, we had a jury and four alternates. The jury consisted of six men and six women; nine of the jurors were black. In order to insulate the jury from any publicity about the case, so as to preserve the defendant's rights to a fair trial, the jury was sequestered at night and during the weekends at a nearby college.

Opening Statements

Except for questions to prospective jurors, the opening statement is the first opportunity the trial attorney has to talk to the jury. In a criminal case, it is the occasion for acquainting the jury with the charges against the defendants and the evidence by which the prosecutor intends to prove those charges. Equally important, it is the major opportunity for establishing some kind of relationship with, or impression on, the jury. Because the prosecution has the burden of proving the charges, it makes the first opening statement.

As I began my opening statement to the jury, I was conscious of the fact that I was facing twelve persons to whom I was a total stranger and who I would ask to find the defendants guilty of serious criminal charges. I must therefore conduct myself in such a manner, in my statements to them and my questioning of the witnesses, that they would feel they could trust me to be fair and not to mislead them. To begin this process, I reminded them of what Judge Gesell had said to them at the start of the trial: that my opening statement was not evidence; that the only evidence in the case would come from persons who would testify from the witness stand and the documents they would present in court; that the defendants were presumed innocent; and that it was the Government's burden to prove beyond a reasonable doubt that they were guilty of the charges against them. I made these statements hoping that the jury would recognize that I fully agreed with what the judge had said, and that I wanted to be fair to the defendants.

I also made it clear that the preview of the evidence that I would give them in the opening statement was for the purpose of showing them "how we would overcome the presumption of innocence and prove beyond a reasonable doubt that the defendants were guilty of the charges against them." I felt that by using these phrases early in the trial, the jury would become accustomed to them and have an easier time understanding and applying them when Judge Gesell gave the jury their instructions and they retired to the jury room to consider the evidence.

Then I reviewed the charges against the defendants as contained in each count of the indictment. Here again, I was careful to point out that, as Judge Gesell had said, the indictment itself was not evidence against the defendants. First, I referred to the individual defendants and advised the jury who they were. In mentioning Ehrlichman, I told the jury that he had previously been advisor to the President for domestic affairs. I described the break-in as "the willful, arrogant act of men who took the law into their own hands because they felt they were above the law."

In order to show the illegality of the break-in, I referred to the Fourth Amendment to the Constitution. As I started to read it, one of Ehrlichman's lawyers objected. I was not sure why the objection was made. The technical basis would have been that I was being argumentative and going beyond a description of the evidence by which I intended to prove the charges. When the objection was made, I was concentrating so intently on what I was saying that it sounded like a voice from another world. I hoped the jury would feel the defense was unfairly trying to keep something from them, so I tried to appear unruffled while at the same time looking as though I could not understand why the defense would interrupt me so impolitely. My effort succeeded when Judge Gesell overruled the objection.

Then I described in detail what Dr. Fielding saw when he was called to his office by the police on that Labor Day weekend of 1971. I wanted the jury to see the physical violence of the break-in right away, and hoped they would remember this scene throughout the trial.

After that, I took them back to the hiring of Howard Hunt in July 1971 and went chronologically through the events and memoranda that led to the break-in. I did this in great detail for almost an hour. I realized that this was a long time to expect the jury to absorb all that I was saying, but I knew they recognized that this was an important case, and I hoped they would understand my effort to give them a complete review of the evidence they would hear. I wanted the jury to hear all the details in advance of the testimony so they could understand the testimony better when they heard it. Also, the more times they heard the details, the better their memories of these details would be when they had to decide the case.

At no time during this lengthy discussion did I make any reference to national security. I hoped that this would make it more difficult for the jury to accept any reference to national security that the defendants might make in their opening statements.

During my discussion of the details, I pointed out that none of those involved had used the term "break-in," and that none of our witnesses would use that term when they testified. Instead, they referred to it as a "surreptitious entry" or a "covert operation." In this connection, when I referred to Krogh's and Young's discussions with Ehrlichman prior to the August 13 memo, I was very general since I was still not certain exactly how Krogh or Young would finally testify on the witness stand. I said:

> They discussed the idea of Hunt and Liddy getting into the Doctor's office in order to examine these files and about Hunt and Liddy's prior experience and professionalism.
>
> And they talked about it in terms of it being covertly—secretly— hidden—concealed—so that no one would ever know it happened—to be in there and out and no one would know it happened, and to be done in a way that could never be traced to or connected in any way with the White House.

I also went into detail about the evidence we would present regarding Ehrlichman's activities in 1973, such as removing the August 11 memo from the file because it was "too sensitive." I characterized these activities as showing "consciousness of guilt." This led into a discussion of the evidence to support the count of lying to the FBI and the three counts of perjury against Ehrlichman. I tried to begin this part of the opening statement gently because here I was, an unknown quantity, accusing John Ehrlichman, one of the President's former top advisers, of lying. I said: "Here I have to say things that are not easy to say about another individual. This is hard to say, but there is no other way to say it; it has to be said—Ehrlichman lied—first to the FBI and then to the grand jury." As I reviewed the perjury charges, I repeated much of the critical evidence that I had already discussed in connection with the count relating to the break-in.

As I ended the opening statement, I tried to give the jury some advance notice that some of the co-conspirators might appear reluctant to testify clearly about specific recollections. I was thinking primarily about Krogh and Young, and I wanted to suggest to the jury that such testimony was probably due to feelings of guilt about being involved in improper conduct. I recognized that such a statement was not strictly related to what we intended to prove, and might be objected to by the defense. However, I felt that it had sufficient bearing on our evidence so that Judge Gesell might overrule any such objection. In any event, it seemed important enough to make the effort, even if the judge sustained the objection. I had only just begun when the objection was made and was sustained. So I was stuck with Krogh and Young and could not do anything to offset the weak testimony that I still feared.

When I concluded, Henry Jones, one of Ehrlichman's black attorneys, gave an opening statement for his client. He admitted that Ehrlichman had approved a "covert operation," but argued that he had not meant to authorize anything illegal. According to Jones, "covert" simply meant "not to be disclosed." Jones also stated that the memos from Young to Ehrlichman that I had described had been altered by Young "to save his own neck" and to implicate Ehrlichman. The jury was also given a preview of Ehrlichman's memory when Jones stated that his client was a busy man and could not be expected to remember all the details of everything that had flowed across his desk at the White House.

The reaction of the press to Ehrlichman's opening statement was to characterize Young as the star witness. I disagreed. I felt that each of our witnesses would be important. If there was any star witness, it would be Ehrlichman and my cross-examination of him. Despite my concern about how Young and Krogh would hold up, I believed our case would be strong enough to overcome the defendants' motions for acquittal at the end of our case. Therefore, Ehrlichman would have to take the stand in his own defense or else face almost certain conviction.

Daniel Schultz, counsel for Barker and Martinez, also gave a short opening statement. He stated he would present evidence that would show his clients had been involved in three other break-ins for the CIA, and that because of this, they believed they were acting legally for the government in the Fielding break-in. Schultz also stressed his clients' loyalty to and belief in Hunt because of their past association in the Bay of Pigs invasion.

Peter Maroulis, Liddy's attorney, took only five minutes to state that his client "reasonably believed that he was authorized to do that which was done. He did not have any intent to do wrong."

Liddy had been described as a secret agent who believed it was still 1950, and that he had been captured and was being held behind enemy lines. We did not expect him to testify in his own defense. Liddy provided his own brand of macabre humor during the trial. He was in the custody of the U.S. marshal because of his jail sentence in the Watergate break-in case. Each morning when he was brought into the courtroom, he would face Ehrlich-man, click his heels, and give the Nazi salute. Ehrlichman would probably have gladly strangled him.

The Prosecution's Case

Prior to the beginning of the trial, we had spent considerable time debating the order of our witnesses. Ultimately, we decided to start strongly with the fact of the break-in through Dr. Fielding. We would bury Young between Hunt and Krogh and put Cathy Chenow (Krogh and Young's former secretary) on immediately after Young because her directness would contrast with Young's equivocation. We felt Krogh should follow rather than precede Young because the stronger testimony we anticipated from Krogh would then help offset the weak testimony we expected from Young.

The opening arguments had taken all morning, so we began our case after lunch. Our first two witnesses were the Beverly Hills policemen who were at the scene of the crime on September 4, 1971. They testified briefly on the legal technicalities necessary to establish the existence of the break-in.

They were followed by Dr. Fielding. The press reported that our case started with the same type of witnesses that would be presented in a normal burglary trial: the investigating officers and the victim. That was exactly how we wanted the jury to perceive the matter.

It is always difficult to predict exactly how a person will react when they testify publicly before a judge and twelve jurors they have never seen before, and in the presence of a crowded courtroom. As a witness, Dr. Fielding was much more nervous than I had expected him to be. I attributed this to the intensity of his dislike of the publicity connected with this affair. His answers were long and rambling. It was difficult for me to keep him on track, and when defense counsel objected to the form of my questions or to a portion of his answer, the doctor had difficulty restraining himself from continuing to talk. At one point, Judge Gesell interrupted to say, "I want to be pleasant with you, but you must stop talking."

Despite this, I was able to take Dr. Fielding through the inquiry by the FBI agents about Ellsberg, and the details of what he had seen in his office on September 4, 1971. I wanted the doctor to tell the jury how he had felt when he saw the shambles in which his office had been left. Under the rules of evidence, I could not ask him a direct question about his "feelings" because this would have been objected to as "irrelevant" and the objection would probably have been sustained. So I tried to word my questions in a way that would help him realize what I was seeking and give him the opportunity of making this answer. If the objection was made and sustained after the answer, at least the jury would have heard what I wanted them to hear. A further problem was that I had to avoid phrasing my questions in a way that appeared to suggest the answer I wanted. Otherwise, the defense could have objected that I was "leading" the witness and suggesting the answer I wanted. My efforts to avoid such objections to the form of my questions, and the doctor's nervousness were too much to overcome. I could not get the kind of answer I had hoped for, and had to end his testimony disappointed that I had been unable to have him convey the same feelings and emotions about the break-in to the trial jury that he had testified about to the grand jury. But I realized that his testimony before the grand jury had been spontaneous, and the fact the he could not intentionally reenact it at the trial was a mark of his integrity.

There was still a little time left in the afternoon, so we called Howard Hunt as our next witness. Hunt testified that it was very likely that he had made the suggestion to break into Dr. Fielding's office. He said he had done so because of the doctor's refusal to talk about Ellsberg to the FBI agents. This made him conclude that a "bag job was in order," and he and Liddy recommended it to Krogh and Young. Hunt also testified about the article regarding Ellsberg's attorney, which Colson had given to a newspaper reporter. With that, court was recessed for the weekend.

We were grateful for the opportunity for further preparation of our witnesses. Much of Saturday was devoted to talking with Young. To my horror, he was almost as bad as when we first talked with him. At one point, he took ten minutes to explain how someone could be in Dr. Fielding's office to examine the records without actually entering the office.

On Monday morning, we finished with Hunt. Among other things, he testified that he and Liddy purchased a glass cutter, a crowbar, and the nylon rope when they stopped in Chicago on their way to California to meet Barker, Martinez, and DeDiego. The first two items helped show that the possibility of a forcible entry was part of their plan.

We spent the balance of the day questioning Young. His testimony was very vague and weak on what he and Krogh told Ehrlichman when they discussed the covert operation with him before writing the August 11 memo. He fenced with me about the definition of the term "break-in." Also, he could not answer whether he considered the fact that persons were in Dr. Fielding's office examining his files without his knowledge or consent to be a violation of the law.

Despite such problems, Young did testify quite well about a telephone call he and Krogh made to Ehrlichman on August 30, after Hunt and Liddy had returned from California. Young said they told Ehrlichman that Hunt and Liddy had returned and that "it looked feasible." Ehrlichman asked if they still recommended that they go ahead. After each responded affirmatively, Ehrlichman said, "Okay, let me know if they find anything."

That telephone call had intrigued us for a long time. During the grand jury investigation, Krogh and Young had described a telephone call they had made to Ehrlichman after Hunt and Liddy had returned from their first trip to California for surveillance of Dr. Fielding's office. They said the telephone call had been made from the White House to Cape Cod, where Ehrlichman was spending the Labor Day weekend with his family. In his testimony before the grand jury, Ehrlichman denied the call, and we were unable to find any record of such a call from the White House or the telephone company.

Young's testimony about Ehrlichman stating that the August 11 memo was too sensitive, and about Ehrlichman's removal of that memo from the file in April 1973, was much stronger and very damaging to Ehrlichman. In this connection, Young testified that he brought the files to Ehrlichman's office in response to a call from Ehrlichman's secretary. Young stated that Ehrlichman's secretary said he did not need to bring the files over right away, because Ehrlichman was out of town. We were able to support Young on this by Ehrlichman's daily log, which showed he was in San Francisco from March 23 to 26.

Young also testified about a meeting with Ehrlichman a few days after the review of the files, in which Ehrlichman described the interview by the FBI regarding Ehrlichman's knowledge of the break-in. According to Young, Ehrlichman said he did not tell the FBI that he had approved of Hunt and Liddy going to California, because the agents had not asked him that question.

Finally, I used Young to get into evidence several other memoranda in addition to the one on August 11. I tried to make it seem like this was the main reason for calling Young as a witness. This helped distract from Young's weak testimony about what Ehrlichman had been told prior to the August 11 memo.

Young's testimony about the documents was null and time-consuming. It resulted in talk among some news reporters attending the trial that we were losing the jury. I had tried enough conspiracy cases that I felt I knew what I was doing and how it would end. In such cases, the evidence comes in one small piece at a time. To a spectator, the testimony of any one witness rarely seems to have been particularly damaging. The extent of the case against the defendants is usually not clear until after all the evidence is in and the prosecutor has gone through the process of fitting all the pieces together in his closing argument. Although I felt certain this would occur in our case, I was disturbed by the apparent negative reaction of some of the reporters. I was relieved when one reporter came up to me during a recess and told me he thought I was handling the case just right, and that I should not worry about what others were saying. He added that most of the other reporters had never seen a real trial and mistakenly thought that every good trial lawyer had to be as flamboyant as Perry Mason on TV.

Each of the memos Young testified about would become an important piece in the final picture we would describe to the jury at the end of the case. In addition to the August 11 memo, there was one dated August 23. It was apparently an agenda for a meeting between Young and Ehrlichman that day, and contained handwriting that Young identified as Ehrlichman's. One of the items listed was "Financing—Special Project No. 1." We believed this meeting was what caused Ehrlichman to ask Colson to come up with $5,000 in cash later in August. Then there was a memo dated August 25 from Young to Ehrlichman, advising Ehrlichman that "Hunt and Liddy have left for California." The next day Young sent another memo to Ehrlichman, which stated that with the release of the article on Ellsberg's lawyer "we have already started on a negative press image for Ellsberg." This memo went on to state: "If the present Hunt/Liddy Project No. 1 is successful, Ehrlichman should talk to Colson about a game plan for using the information obtained." Young attached a draft of a memo for Ehrlichman to send to Colson, which stated: "On the assumption that the proposed undertaking by Hunt and Liddy would be carried out, and would be successful, I would appreciate receiving from you, by next Wednesday, a game plan as to how and when you believe the materials should be used." Ehrlichman sent such a memo to Colson on August 27.

After Young, we called Cathy Chenow, who had been the secretary for Young and Krogh in the Plumbers' office at the Executive Office Building.

She testified about typing the break-in memo from Hunt and Liddy after their first trip to California to stake out Dr. Fielding's office. She also described saying something to Liddy as to whether ordinary people would go to jail for doing what was described in the memo. According to her, Liddy responded, "Yes, but as long as it's being done for the Government no one will ever find out."

Then we called Krogh and spent the rest of the day questioning him. The contrast between Krogh and Young was electrifying. Krogh's answers were direct, positive, and decisive. They were devastating to Ehrlichman. I attributed the difference in their answers to their differing reactions to testifying publicly. Young had not been able to face the fact that what he had done was wrong; he still had something to hide, or to hide from. Krogh had nothing to hide; he had been able to admit his guilt, and wanted to help prevent similar wrongdoing in the future.

With Krogh, I intentionally deferred any discussion about the August 11 memo and its meaning, or the meeting with Ehrlichman prior to August 11 where the proposed covert operation was discussed. I wanted to take him through what led up to this, not just in order to review what had occurred chronologically, but primarily to commit him to a foundation from which it would be difficult to believe that Ehrlichman did not know exactly what was being proposed. So I started with the discussions Krogh and Young had with Hunt and Liddy after Dr. Fielding had refused to talk with the FBI about Ellsberg. I brought Young's name into my questions as often as possible, because I hoped Krogh's answers would be stronger than Young's and this would make Young's testimony seem stronger than it had actually been.

Krogh testified that Hunt and Liddy had said they had the ability to obtain whatever information Dr. Fielding had in his files about Ellsberg. He said that although the term "break-in" was not used, it was clear that Hunt and Liddy were talking about going into Dr. Fielding's office without his knowledge or consent. Krogh then testified that he and Young met with Ehrlichman on August 5 to discuss the matter further. According to Krogh, they met with Ehrlichman because they realized they could not approve such an operation on their own; they needed Ehrlichman's approval. Krogh remembered Ehrlichman saying something at that meeting about it not being traceable. I covered the fact that the word "break-in" was not used—I did not want to leave this for the defense to ask. But I stressed that an entry into Dr. Fielding's office was contemplated. The crucial questions and answers were:

> MERRILL: Did you authorize an entry, Mr. Krogh?
> KROGH: Yes.
> MERRILL: Did you believe you had authorization?
> KROGH: Yes.
> MERRILL: On what did you base that belief?
> KROGH: I based it on the discussions with Mr. Ehrlichman. I based it on the memorandum.
> MERRILL: What memorandum?
> KROGH: The August 11 memorandum. And on the final telephone call.
> MERRILL: What call?
> KROGH: The August 30, 1971 telephone call.

Krogh's reference to the August 30 telephone call to Ehrlichman, when Ehrlichman was vacationing on Cape Cod, corroborated Young's testimony on this matter. The more support we could develop for Young's testimony, the tougher it would be for Ehrlichman.

Krogh testified that when he told Ehrlichman about the break-in after it had occurred, Ehrlichman was very critical of what had been done. I wanted the jury to realize that Ehrlichman was upset about how the examination of the files had been carried out, and not about the fact that the files had been examined. He was upset because it was no longer "covert" or "not traceable." So I asked if Ehrlichman said anything about not having expected anyone to be in the doctor's office to look at the files. He said, "No."

Krogh also testified that after the break-in, he told Ehrlichman of Hunt and Liddy's suggestion that they break into Dr. Fielding's apartment. He said he recommended against this, and that Ehrlichman agreed with him.

On cross-examination, William Frates, Ehrlichman's chief trial attorney, asked Krogh if the word "break-in" was used during the August 30 telephone call. Krogh replied, "No, sir."

This gave me the opportunity to ask Krogh more about the call, and on redirect examination, he explained that Ehrlichman was talking on a public phone and that he and Young did not state specifically what they were recommending, so that no one would overhear them. He testified:

> It was an open telephone line. I was doing my best to convey to him that conditions had been met that this would be nontraceable. This was not something I wanted overheard by anyone.
>
> I don't recall using the term "entry." However, we had used terms of "operation," "effort," and "covert" which embraced what took place.

There was one other matter I had to cover with Krogh. When he had resigned as undersecretary of transportation in May 1973, his letter to Nixon had stated that the Fielding break-in was "my responsibility, a step taken in excess of instructions, and without knowledge or permission of any superior."

Technically this was correct—no one had approved a "break-in," which by its very nature is not covert and could be traceable. But I could not avoid this letter and leave it for the defense to cover. They might improperly exaggerate it, or create the impression that I had not referred to it because it was damaging to Krogh. So I asked Krogh about this in order that the jury would not suspect I was trying to hide anything from them. Krogh's response was terrific:

> I felt, at that time, that it was necessary for me to affirm my responsibility regardless of what other individuals had done or not done.
>
> I thought I would leave to others what they felt appropriate for themselves.

Krogh's final blows to Ehrlichman were his answers regarding discussions with Ehrlichman in March and April 1973. He testified about a telephone call from Ehrlichman near the end of March in which Ehrlichman stated that Hunt "might be going public about the Fielding break-in." Krogh met with Ehrlichman the next day, and Ehrlichman suggested that Krogh ought to try to obtain some kind of immunity from prosecution for what had happened. According to Krogh, Ehrlichman also mentioned at that meeting the possibility of claiming that Hunt and Liddy were responsible for the break-in on their own, and that no one else knew about or approved it. Krogh said Ehrlichman phoned him the next day and said, "Hang tough." Near the end of April, Ehrlichman phoned again and told Krogh he had been interviewed by the FBI about the break-in and had to "dissemble" to them.

On Wednesday, we finished with Krogh and called Colson, the man from whom he had obtained the $5,000 in cash for Hunt and Liddy's expenses, and then General Cushman.

Colson began his testimony by describing the hiring of Howard Hunt. He testified that when Hunt was hired, he (Colson) told Ehrlichman that Hunt had said he would need some help from the CIA. Colson then described obtaining the $5,000 at Ehrlichman's request. Colson had a clear recollection of the request. He remembered that Ehrlichman was away for the Labor Day weekend and phoned Colson at the White House and asked him to get this money for Krogh. Colson resented the fact that everyone else had been able to get away, but he was stuck in Washington. This helped corroborate Young's and Krogh's testimony about their phone call to Ehrlichman on Cape Cod. I asked Colson if Ehrlichman said what the money was for. He said, "No." Colson also testified about releasing Hunt's derogatory article about Ellsberg's attorney. He said he did so in response to a request from the President. Colson also described the roundabout manner in which the money was paid, also in cash.

General Cushman testified about his meeting with Hunt in July 1971. Despite his memos in December 1972 about not remembering who called him regarding Hunt, he testified that the call was from Ehrlichman. By using the CIA transcript of the meeting with Hunt, which referred to a previous call from Ehrlichman, I had refreshed the general's recollection sufficiently so that he no longer had any doubts about who had called him.

We introduced into evidence the transcript of that meeting. This would make it more difficult for Ehrlichman to deny any such call.

The general then testified about calling Ehrlichman on August 27, 1971, and stating that the CIA would not provide any further help for Hunt. He said he told Ehrlichman that he thought Hunt was involving the Agency in surveillance of an American citizen (which was beyond its statutory jurisdiction), and that Hunt had questionable judgment.

General Cushman also testified about the phone calls from Ehrlichman in December 1972, and the memos the general wrote at that time about the first call regarding Hunt. I did not ask him if Ehrlichman influenced him in any way in the writing of these memos. I decided that I would later argue to the jury that Ehrlichman had been responsible for these memos, and that this showed Ehrlichman's consciousness of guilt.

In asking the general about the December 1972 memos, I recognized that I would be running a risk because of the apparent inconsistency in what he had just testified to about the initial call about Hunt being from Ehrlichman. However, it seemed that this risk was minimal because Ehrlichman's counsel would not try to exploit the apparent inconsistency for fear that to do so would emphasize Ehrlichman's role and motive in causing the December 1972 memos to be written.

We also called the FBI agent who interviewed Ehrlichman, and the court reporter who had transcribed his grand jury testimony. This laid the basis for the statements we claimed were false in the last four counts of the indictment.

Court recessed early that afternoon because the next day was Independence Day. After the jury had retired, I stated that we had no further evidence and would rest our case at the opening of court on Friday. I spent the Fourth preparing for Ehrlichman's cross-examination.

Defendants' Case

At the conclusion of our case, the defense asked the Court to dismiss the charges against their clients on the grounds that the Special Prosecutor had not presented sufficient evidence from which the jury could find each defendant guilty of the charges beyond a reasonable doubt. After hearing brief arguments, Judge Gesell denied the motions. Now Ehrlichman would have to testify.

Ehrlichman began his defense by calling two former secretaries, the CIA psychiatrist who had prepared the psychological profile on Ellsberg, and three character witnesses who did not feel this testimony was of any substance or had any real bearing on the issues before the jury. The secretaries simply stated that Ehrlichman was a very busy man. The CIA witness and the reference to the psychological profile on Ellsberg was an effort to raise the cloud of national security, but I did not feel it could be used as the basis for an argument justifying the break-in.

After the character witnesses testified about Ehrlichman's good reputation, they were cross-examined as to whether they thought Ehrlichman's reputation would be the same if it was known that he had authorized a break-in or lied to the grand jury. Merely asking the question was enough to neutralize their testimony.

Court recessed for the weekend, and I spent all day Saturday and Sunday preparing to cross-examine Ehrlichman.

On Monday morning, Ehrlichman took the stand in his own defense. His wife and five children were in the front row of the spectator seats. Much time was taken up by Ehrlichman's attorney asking questions about his personal background and his work at the White House. The latter elicited Ehrlichman's concern over the Pentagon Papers and the leak of classified information in 1971. When I objected that these matters were not involved in this trial, Judge Gesell suggested that Ehrlichman's attorney get on to matters in which the jury was interested. With that, Ehrlichman's testimony was concluded rather quickly by a series of direct questions in which he denied authorizing any break-in, being aware of any psychological profile, removing any memos from the files, or lying to the FBI or grand jury. His defense was that he thought the August 11 memo referred to a conventional, legal investigation. He tried to defuse the effect of the other memos that we had introduced into evidence by describing how busy he was, and stating that he intentionally trained himself not to clutter up his mind with all the details of things that crossed his desk. He testified that when Krogh told him about the break-in after it happened, he was very critical of what had been done. He also produced a transcript of a telephone call he made to Krogh about being interviewed by the FBI. The transcript did not contain the word "dissemble."

Ehrlichman's attorney tried to get into evidence his notes relating to meetings with the President. I objected, and the judge dismissed the jury so we could argue the point. Ehrlichman's argument was that the notes showed that the President had not ordered the break-in. Judge Gesell reminded the defense that no one had claimed the President ordered the break-in, and sustained our objection.

Just before lunch, I began my cross-examination. As always during the trial, lunch consisted of sandwiches and milk in an office at the courthouse, during which Bakes, Breyer, and I discussed our strategy. My strategy with Ehrlichman was to show that he had a very selective memory. He remembered many details of matters that were not incriminating, but could not remember anything about the incriminating matters that had been testified to by others. This also would make it possible for me to show that according to Ehrlichman, each of our witnesses was either mistaken or lying, and that only Ehrlichman was telling the truth. So it could not be Ehrlichman against just Young, as his lawyers had said in their opening argument, but Ehrlichman against Hunt, Young, Krogh, and Colson.

I started with the August 11 memo, since this was the most incriminating evidence against him. Although Ehrlichman denied he had authorized a break-in, he had some difficulty answering my questions regarding what he understood "covert" to mean, or what he meant by "not traceable," or why he wanted this to be "not traceable." At one point, Ehrlichman testified that he thought the examination of the files could be done with the doctor's consent, but he never explained how this could be done and still be "covert" and "not traceable."

Then I went into the meeting with Krogh and Young that preceded the August 11 memo. Ehrlichman's log showed a meeting with Krogh and

Young at 11:30 on August 5. Krogh and Young had testified that this was the meeting where they discussed with Ehrlichman the examination of the files in Dr. Fielding's office. They also said this meeting followed one where the three of them met with Melvin Laird and Fred Buzhardt. I asked Ehrlichman what he recalled of the meeting with Laird and Buzhardt, and to my surprise he testified about several details regarding that meeting. I had expected that he would say he did not recall anything, and I would be faced with trying to persuade the jury that his repeated lack of any recollection showed he was not telling the truth. He apparently felt that his testimony about not remembering what Krogh and Young said they discussed with him might be more believable to the jury if he appeared cooperative and told them about some things he could remember.

It was the same tack he had tried before the grand jury. I felt encouraged. This approach had failed completely before the grand jury. I recognized that if I could put enough situations before the trial jury in which Ehrlichman could remember some innocent and relatively meaningless details but said he was unable to remember the incriminating details testified to by Young, Krogh, and Colson, then the jury would not believe Ehrlichman's denial of any knowledge that someone was going to be in Dr. Fielding's office to look at the files. This would also influence the jury in its consideration of the perjury charges.

We went on to the other memos. When I questioned him about the August 23 memo, Ehrlichman said he could not remember meeting with Young and talking about financing for the Hunt/Liddy Project No. 1. To my surprise, he admitted that this project included the examination of Dr. Fielding's files.

In cross-examining Ehrlichman about General Cushman's testimony, I began with the phone call on August 27, 1971, when Cushman said the CIA could no longer provide help to Hunt. I started there because I knew he would admit to remembering that call. However, his answers were rather curious. When I asked what he said to Cushman, he replied that he merely asked whether Hunt worked for the CIA or for the White House, as though he did not know why Cushman had called him. I felt I could make this seem unbelievable in my closing argument. To nail it down, I asked him if he had asked Krogh what Hunt was doing at the CIA after receiving this call from Cushman. He said, "No."

In connection with the rest of Cushman's testimony, Ehrlichman said he could not recall phoning the general about Hunt in July 1971, or phoning him about any memos in December 1972. I confronted him with the fact that in an early appearance before the grand jury, in May 1973, he had testified that he was "morally certain" that he had not called Cushman about Hunt in July 1971. Then I called his attention to Cushman's testimony about the call, Colson's testimony about Hunt's request for help from the CIA, and the transcript of the meeting between Hunt and Cushman in which Cushman referred to a call from Ehrlichman. In the face of this, I got him to admit that his previous "morally certain" testimony must have been incorrect. I felt this would be very damaging to Ehrlichman because I was quite sure the judge would use the term "moral certainty" in his charge to the jury in connection with reasonable doubt.

We went on to the telephone call to him on Cape Cod that Krogh and Young had testified to, and the one Colson said he received from him "on vacation" at the end of August. To each question, Ehrlichman said he did not remember any such call.

I had to do something with Ehrlichman's testimony regarding being critical of what happened after Krogh told him about the break-in. So I got him to repeat how critical he had been, which he did in very strong terms. Then I asked him a series of questions that I hoped would reveal that such criticism was about how the operation had been carried out, and not because they had been in Dr. Fielding's office:

MERRILL: Did you report this to the Beverly Hills police?
EHRLICHMAN: No.
MERRILL: Did you report it to the Justice Department?
EHRLICHMAN: No.
MERRILL: Did you fire Mr. Hunt?
EHRLICHMAN: No.

MERRILL: Did you fire Mr. Liddy?

EHRLICHMAN: No.

MERRILL: Did you fire Mr. Young?

EHRLICHMAN: No.

MERRILL: Did you fire Mr. Krogh?

EHRLICHMAN: No.

MERRILL: Did you tell the President?

EHRLICHMAN: No.

MERRILL: Did you write a memo or ask anyone to write a memo about what had happened and your criticism of it?

EHRLICHMAN: No.

Ehrlichman said he did not remember Krogh telling him that Hunt and Liddy suggested they break into Dr. Fielding's apartment. Under further questioning, Ehrlichman said he could not remember suggesting that Krogh try to obtain immunity from prosecution for the break-in, or that he had ever told Krogh that he had to dissemble to the FBI.

To support Young's testimony about the removal of the August 11 memo from the Plumbers' files, and to provide further evidence of Ehrlichman's perjury, I asked him about his production of a copy of the August 11 memo to a Senate committee. He testified that he did this after reading in the newspaper that the original Watergate prosecutors had a copy of such a memo. This was the copy they had obtained from Young. Ehrlichman explained that he went to the White House and "found a copy of the memo in my files."

We had fenced with each other on a few points, but each time I felt I came out ahead. As an example, on one occasion when I asked him about a particular meeting, he said he did not remember it and, as if to make light of his answer, added that for all he knew there could have been an elephant in his office that day. I responded sarcastically that I had not asked about an elephant, but about a specific meeting with certain people where a particular subject was discussed.

When Ehrlichman's cross-examination was over, I felt I had covered everything I had intended and that his answers had not detracted from the evidence that, I would later argue to the jury, showed he was guilty of the charges against him beyond a reasonable doubt. My colleagues and I agreed that there would be no need to ask Ehrlichman any further questions, no matter what his own attorney asked him on redirect examination.

The redirect was short and uneventful. It ended with Ehrlichman attempting to explain that the reason he did not report the break-in to the Beverly Hills Police or the Justice Department was because the President had said it was a matter of national security and that no one should talk about it. This was not going to help him very much, since the written interrogatories to the President that would be part of the evidence before the jury showed that the President said he was not aware of the Fielding break-in until March 1973. So obviously, the President could not have issued such instructions for more than a year and a half after the break-in. I decided not to question Ehrlichman any further about this, and to cover it in my closing argument to the jury.

However, on an impulse, as his attorney sat down, I rose, and without going to the lectern said: "Mr. Ehrlichman, isn't the reason you did not report the break-in to the Beverly Hills Police or the Justice Department was because that would have made it no longer covert or not traceable?"

Ehrlichman reacted as though he had been hit on the head with a wooden mallet. He stared at me, almost blindly, for a long moment. His lower jaw dropped as though it was suddenly unhinged. He started to answer, stopped, and started again. Then he said, "I don't know how to answer that question."

I did not want to spoil the effect on the jury by trying to help him, so I said, "I have no further questions" and sat down.

From Ehrlichman's dark and brooding appearance after his cross-examination, it seemed to me that he recognized he was going to be convicted. I was surprised the next day during a short recess when he came up to me, held out his hand, smiled, and said: "Mr. Merrill, I want to congratulate you on a very thorough but fair cross-examination." I was embarrassed, thinking of what I had done to him in front of his wife and children, and of the effect on all of them of the jury verdict of guilty I was sure would come. As I shook his hand, I mumbled something about being sorry that our meeting had been under such circumstances.

Ehrlichman's attorney then called Henry Kissinger as a witness. This was an effort to impeach Young as to whether Kissinger's name had been used in connection with the request for the CIA profile on Ellsberg. I felt the reason was to raise the specter of national security, and perhaps to make Ehrlichman the beneficiary of Kissinger's good reputation. Although it seemed technically improper to allow such testimony, I recognized that Judge Gesell was bending over backwards to be fair to the defendants. Kissinger's testimony was almost meaningless to the jury, and certainly harmless to our case. I felt we should not ask any questions, in order to minimize his testimony and avoid opening up any areas relating to national security. But one of my associates asked one innocuous question. Kissinger was on and off the witness stand in about two minutes.

In rebuttal, we called three witnesses who had custody of the files at the White House. Through them, we brought out that the originals of three of the critical memos were found in Ehrlichman's personal files:

- the August 11 memo, recommending the examination of the files and containing Ehrlichman's approval;
- the August 25 memo, stating that "Hunt and Liddy have left for California"; and
- the August 26 memo, suggesting that Ehrlichman send a memo to Colson for developing a game plan "if the present Hunt/Liddy Project No. 1 is successful."

Barker testified that he had been approached by Howard Hunt in the summer of 1971. According to Barker, Hunt said he was working at the White House and asked if Barker would become "operational again" and help with a surreptitious entry to obtain information on a "traitor." Hunt said the FBI could not become involved, because of recent Court decisions, and the CIA did not have jurisdiction over such a matter. Barker relayed this information

to Martinez. Both Barker and Martinez testified about their prior association with the CIA, particularly with Hunt in connection with the Bay of Pigs
invasion. Their testimony was that the general instructions they received
from Hunt for the Fielding break-in were similar to instructions they had
received from Hunt or others in the CIA on previous occasions. They said
they were relying on what they believed was Hunt's authority.

On cross-examination, we brought out that both Barker and Martinez
had been American citizens and were, therefore, aware of the Constitution.
Barker stated that a "surreptitious entry" was the same thing as a "covert
operation." He added that it had been planned to be covert so no one would
know about it. Martinez admitted that the break-in might have been illegal
for a "normal citizen."

Liddy did not take the stand or offer any witnesses on his behalf.

Testimony was concluded around noon. After lunch, the President's
answers to the written questions submitted to him were read to the jury. We
did not feel they helped the defendants. Nixon said he had not authorized
the examination of the files in Dr. Fielding's office, and that he first learned
of it in March 1973.

Court adjourned early to enable counsel to put the finishing touches on
their closing arguments the following day.

Closing Arguments

In a criminal case, the prosecution is allowed to make two closing arguments to the jury before and after the defendants' arguments. This is
because the prosecution has the burden of proving the defendants guilty
beyond a reasonable doubt. The first argument is generally limited to a
recitation of the facts. The second is used to reply to the arguments made
by the defendants.

I began my first argument by thanking the jury for being so attentive,
and for enduring the inconvenience of having been sequestered. I reminded
them that our system of justice could not function if citizens did not accept

the responsibility of jury service. In order to avoid seeming presumptuous, or offending them by telling them how they should decide the case, I reminded them that what I would say was not evidence. I said: "In the last analysis, it is your recollection, collective recollections that will be important. But we are engaged here in a mutual search for the truth; and, therefore, let me then review this with you."

For the next hour and a quarter, I reviewed the evidence as I saw it.

First, I discussed the conspiracy count against all defendants. This was for violating Dr. Fielding's civil rights under the Fourth Amendment by searching his files without his knowledge or consent. Discussing this count first would make it easier to discuss the perjury charges against Ehrlichman alone later. I pointed out that there was, of course, no written agreement between the conspirators, but that we had proved the existence of the conspiracy by showing the defendants' common course of action. In the discussion of this count, I started with Barker, Martinez, and Liddy because the evidence against them clearly established the fact of the break-in. I felt this would make my description of the evidence of Ehrlichman's advance knowledge of the operation more damaging to Ehrlichman.

In this connection, I reminded the jury that we had not charged a break-in. This was necessary because of what I expected Ehrlichman's attorney would say. I said:

> In this recitation of the evidence, I think you should bear in mind what the main issue is in this case. The main issue is: Who was aware of a plan to search Dr. Fielding's files? The issue in this case is not: Who was aware of a break-in, because a break-in was not what was originally planned. A break-in occurred when Mr. Barker and Mr. Martinez and Mr. DeDiego found the door was locked. But a break-in was not originally planned.
>
> All that was planned in the beginning was a covert operation that no one would know about, to examine the Doctor's files in his office.

After briefly reviewing the highlights of the chronology, I repeated the evidence against Barker, Martinez, and Liddy. It did not seem that there could be any question in the minds of the jury that Barker, Martinez, and Liddy had been part of a plan to enter Dr. Fielding's office illegally. In order not to leave any doubt, I repeated Cathy Chenow's question, "Wouldn't ordinary people go to jail for something like this?" The final piece of evidence regarding Liddy that I mentioned was his recommendation (with Hunt) that they "knock off" the doctor's apartment.

Then I started on the evidence against Ehrlichman. I began with the meeting where Hunt and Liddy told Krogh and Young of the need to examine Dr. Fielding's files because he would not talk with the FBI about Ellsberg. This evidence showed that these four clearly understood that someone would have to be in Dr. Fielding's office in order to examine his files. It supported the testimony of Krogh and Young that they thought they had made Ehrlichman fully aware of what was proposed. I emphasized that it was necessary for Krogh and Young to talk with Ehrlichman about this, because they could not approve it on their own. I also stressed that no one used the word "break-in," because a break-in would not be "covert" or "not traceable." Then I read to the jury the August 11 memo, including Ehrlichman's approval and his hand-written note: "If done under your assurance that is not traceable."

I reminded the jury of Ehrlichman's testimony that he thought the examination could be done with the doctor's consent, and pointed out that this was inconsistent with the testimony of Krogh and Young, and with the use of the words "covert" and "not traceable" in the August 11 memo. I said: "If you try to get the doctor's consent to look at his files, he is obviously going to know about it and it will no longer be covert or not traceable."

Next, I discussed in detail the other memos that connected Ehrlichman with the operation. This led to the August 27 telephone call from General Cushman to Ehrlichman in which the general said he told Ehrlichman that the CIA would no longer help Hunt. Ehrlichman had testified that he asked Cushman whether Hunt was working for the White House or the CIA. I repeated this testimony and showed how inconceivable it was by listing the evidence that proved Ehrlichman knew Hunt was working for the White House:

- The August 5 meeting with Krogh and Young.
- The August 11 memo about the covert operation.
- The August 23 memo about funds for the Special Project.
- The August 25 memo about Hunt and Liddy leaving for California.
- The August 26 memo about the necessity for a game plan.

My argument on this incriminating aspect of Ehrlichman's testimony continued:

Despite this call from General Cushman and the things that General Cushman said about concern about the Agency being involved in the surveillance of an American citizen or the possibility of Hunt having questionable judgment, despite this, Mr. Ehrlichman admitted he did not ask Mr. Krogh: What is Hunt doing? What do you think of his judgment? Nor did he ask that Hunt be ordered to come back from California. Even though by then he would have had to know, because he received the August 25 memo.

Instead, what did Mr. Ehrlichman do? Even after that warning from General Cushman?

Ehrlichman sent the August 27 memorandum to Mr. Colson, asking him to draw up a game plan for the use of this information. . . .

And Ehrlichman talked to Colson, from Colson's own testimony, about funds for Krogh.

This took us to the testimony of Krogh and Young about the August 30 telephone call to Ehrlichman on Cape Cod after Hunt and Liddy returned from their surveillance of Dr. Fielding's office. I pointed out how this evidence was corroborated by Colson's testimony regarding the call from Ehrlichman to get $5,000 in cash for Krogh and Young. I tried to nail this down further:

Colson also testified to something significant. He said Mr. Ehrlichman didn't tell him what the money was for.

Now, if the operation was innocent or legal, then why didn't Mr. Ehrlichman tell Mr. Colson what the money was for?

Mr. Ehrlichman has only said he couldn't remember talking about funds to Mr. Colson.

I had to dispose of Ehrlichman's testimony that he was angry when Krogh told him what had occurred. I did this by repeating Krogh's explanation of his own feelings, and by playing down Ehrlichman's reaction:

What did Krogh say he felt? Mr. Krogh said he was surprised and upset because they had exceeded his instructions; and that they had exceeded his instructions by causing this damage, by breaking in, so that it was now going to be evident that somebody had been in the Doctor's office.

Mr. Krogh said he was upset because it wasn't covert and that is what it was supposed to have been. He was afraid that now it might even become traceable to the White House, because somebody might connect up the fact that the Doctor had been asked to talk to the FBI near the end of July, and then his office had been broken into the first part of September.

However, Mr. Krogh also testified—and this is significant—that he was not surprised that someone had been in the Doctor's office to examine the files, because Mr. Krogh said, that is what Mr. Ehrlichman had approved. He felt that is what Mr. Ehrlichman had approved because that is what they had talked about on the August 5 meeting; that is what they had recommended in the August 11 memorandum; and what Mr. Ehrlichman had approved in the August 11 memorandum; and that is what they talked about on the telephone on August 30.

Then Mr. Krogh told Mr. Ehrlichman, and what was his reaction? The same as Mr. Krogh's. He was upset, too, because they hadn't followed the instructions. It wasn't covert and it might now be traceable.

However, he did not tell Mr. Krogh at that time that he had not expected anyone to be in the Doctor's office to look at the files.

I also contrasted Ehrlichman's testimony about his reaction to what had happened with his testimony about not reporting the break-in. I reminded the jury of Ehrlichman's inability to answer my final question about not reporting the break-in because that would have made it no longer covert or not traceable. I said:

> He didn't report it to the Justice Department.
> He did not fire Mr. Hunt.
> He did not fire Mr. Liddy.
> He didn't fire Mr. Young.
> He didn't fire Mr. Krogh.
> He didn't tell the President.
> He didn't even write a memorandum or ask anyone to write a memorandum about what had happened.
>
> Mr. Ehrlichman cannot, obviously, say that he failed to do any of these things because he was under any order of the President, because from the President's interrogatories, which were read to you yesterday, the President has said he was not aware of the break-in until March of 1973. So he could hardly have told Mr. Ehrlichman not to talk about it, since he didn't even know about it.

Then I reviewed Ehrlichman's attempts to cover up the fact of the break-in and his approval of the examination of the files, which I characterized as evidence showing "consciousness of guilt." I used this term to describe what Ehrlichman had done, because I knew the judge would use the same terminology in his charge to the jury. Here I discussed the phone calls to General Cushman in December 1972, the memos concerning the first call regarding Hunt, the suggestion to Krogh in March 1973 that he try to get some kind of immunity, the removal from the file in March 1973 of the memos he described to Young as being "too sensitive," Krogh's testimony that Ehrlichman said he had had to "dissemble" to the FBI in April 1973, and Young's testimony that Ehrlichman said he did not tell the FBI he had approved of Hunt and Liddy going to California because they had not asked him that question. I explained that "dissemble" meant "to conceal with intent to deceive." I also pointed out that the transcript of the telephone conversation that Ehrlichman had placed in evidence was for a different date from that testified to by Krogh, so the fact that Ehrlichman's transcript did not contain the word "dissemble" was meaningless and merely an effort to confuse the jury.

This led naturally to the evidence that proved Ehrlichman had lied to the FBI about not seeing the file for over a year, and to the grand jury about not being aware of the psychological profile on Ellsberg, not being aware of the effort to obtain information from Ellsberg's psychiatrist, and about not being aware of the location of the Plumbers' files. I reviewed the testimony of Young, which showed Ehrlichman had reviewed the files less than two months before he was interviewed by the FBI. I described the six memos and testimony by Krogh and Young that showed Ehrlichman was aware of the psychological profile. I repeated the testimony about the August 5 meeting with Krogh and Young, the telephone call to Colson for the cash, and five memoranda that showed he had known of the effort to obtain information from Dr. Fielding's files.

I had planned to make a vivid, dramatic closing summary of my argument by drawing red circles on 3' × 4' enlargements of calendars for July, August, and September 1971 of those dates when Ehrlichman had testified he did not recall something about which one of our witnesses had testified. As I did this, I explained the particular piece of evidence that was involved. When I concluded, there were red circles around July 7, 27, and 30; August 2, 5, 11, 12, 23, 25, 26, 27, 30, and 31; and September 7. Verbally, I added his failure to recall matters testified to by our witnesses relating to March 21, 27; April 27, 30; and May 1, 14, 1973.

I ended my argument by pointing out to the jury that only Ehrlichman said he did not know a surreptitious entry was going to occur in Dr. Fielding's office. I contrasted this with those who knew: Barker, Martinez, DeDiego, Hunt, Liddy, Chenow, Krogh, and Young. I stated that this fact, plus all the evidence I had reviewed, showed that all the defendants were guilty beyond a reasonable doubt of all the charges against them.

William Frates, Ehrlichman's chief trial counsel, argued that his client did not know an illegal entry into Dr. Fielding's office was planned. He tried to defend Ehrlichman's inability to remember certain details regarding meetings, phone calls, and memoranda by describing how busy Ehrlichman had been as the President's advisor for domestic affairs. Frates referred to Young as a man who could not give a straight answer to any question asked. He also argued that Ehrlichman had been tricked into the answers he had given to certain questions before the grand jury, which led to the perjury counts in the indictment.

Liddy's attorney argued briefly that his client had simply been following orders and thought the plan was legal.

Daniel Schultz, counsel for Barker and Martinez, argued that they were the innocent victims of a "cruel fraud" by Howard Hunt. He carried this sympathy argument further by pointing out that Hunt had been given immunity, while Barker and Martinez had been prosecuted. He stressed his clients' prior service for the country working for the CIA. Schultz stated that any danger to the personal liberty of Americans through illegal entries came from "people in power who abuse that power" and not from "these two little men from Miami." Referring to their imprisonment for the Watergate break-in, he said his clients "have been victimized enough already in this sorry chapter in our history."

In my final argument, I pointed out how each of the defendants was attacking someone—Ellsberg, the CIA, our witnesses, and even the special prosecutors—instead of answering the facts that related to that witness's involvement. Then I tried to answer most of the specific arguments made by the defendants' lawyers regarding particular matters that had been testified to.

As for the argument that Ehrlichman was very busy, I had noticed that there was an inked-in comma in the August 27 memo that Ehrlichman sent to Colson about the game plan for the use of any information obtained by Hunt and Liddy. I had intentionally refrained from raising this previously. Now I suggested that the jury could conclude that he was not too busy to have time to read that memo so carefully that he added the comma.

Again, I stressed Ehrlichman's selective memory, and repeated those occasions that illustrated his remembering things that were not harmful to him but not recalling things that could be incriminating. As an example, I reminded the jury of the details that Ehrlichman had testified to, remembering about his first meeting with Hunt. I said:

> The first one, let's talk about this date of July the 7th. Mr. Ehrlichman testified about a detailed discussion he had with Mr. Hunt, along with Mr. Colson. You may remember, the details were simply amazing.
>
> Mr. Colson told him about Hunt's career with the CIA; that Hunt had been in China; that Hunt had experience as an author and had written books and novels and mysteries. And Colson said that Hunt was going to determine the accuracy of the Pentagon Papers.
>
> A fantastic memory. And yet, on that same date, he could not recall a telephone call to General Cushman. He said he was "morally certain."
>
> The reason that that call is significant is, of course, because it connects Mr. Ehrlichman with some of the assistance that was used by Hunt at Dr. Fielding's office; and that is an element that would be traceable.

I repeated that no one had approved in advance a physical breaking-in of the door of the doctor's office, and added that "Everyone, including Mr. Ehrlichman, knew and contemplated that there would be an examination of the files by someone being in the office to look at those files."

Then I tried to anticipate what Judge Gesell would say in his instructions to the jury about national security. Referring to something the judge said would help give credibility to other things I said. As for national security, I said:

> National security is no defense, as His Honor will charge you. It is no defense, no legal defense to violating the Fourth Amendment to our Constitution.
>
> There is nothing in the evidence to show Dr. Fielding was a threat to national security. He was an ordinary, innocent American citizen.

If going into Dr. Fielding's office, as was done here, can be justified on grounds of national security, then God save this nation from such security.

I had to counteract the plea for sympathy by Schultz on behalf of Barker and Martinez. If they were acquitted, this might cause the jury to have some doubts about Ehrlichman. If they were convicted, the jury could not possibly acquit Ehrlichman. I said:

Mr. Barker and Mr. Martinez are mistaken when they talk about marching to a different drum. In this country, we must all march to the drum of the Constitution. There are no exceptions.

Perhaps they are entitled to some sympathy. Maybe they feel they were misled. But defrauded? We are talking about grown men. They weren't ordered to do this; and they aren't the ones who were injured.

Dr. Fielding was the one who was injured. More than that, the American people were injured in this. Our Constitution is the victim.

The misuse of national security that Mr. Schultz talked about is true; but they are not the only ones that are accused of misusing it. The misuse of national security is from the top on down; and the only way to stop it is to hold all of those that were involved in this responsible and liable for their actions.

We didn't object to the reference to Mr. Barker's medals because we didn't want to keep anything from you. But surely Mr. Schultz isn't contending that just because Mr. Barker had honorable wartime service, that gives him a license to violate the civil rights of the rest of us.

The irony is that Mr. Barker and Mr. Martinez didn't even know the name Ellsberg. It didn't mean anything to them. And yet they went into this Doctor's office anyhow.

The further irony of Mr. Barker's testimony is what he talked about as to what had happened to him in Cuba, as to his own civil rights, and then what he ended up doing here to Dr. Fielding.

Mr. Barker and Mr. Martinez are both citizens. They know the Constitution. Mr. Martinez said something about he recognized this would be illegal for ordinary citizens. Since when did he become something different than an ordinary citizen with anything more than the same rights and responsibilities that the rest of us have?

There is no evidence that the CIA approved this break-in. The evidence is all to the contrary.

There is no evidence that anyone told Barker or Martinez that the CIA approved it. And there is certainly no evidence that anyone told Barker or Martinez that they had the approval of any legal authority to do this. They simply thought they did.

It should not matter what they thought, whether they thought it was approved by the CIA or the FBI or the White House. It is wrong and it cannot be justified.

If we are to continue to have a country in which individual rights and freedoms are to be safe and secure, people simply cannot be allowed to violate these rights because they are told by somebody else that it is O.K.

I concluded by trying to contrast what had been done to Dr. Fielding to the principle of law embodied in the Fourth Amendment.

The principle of individual responsibility under the law must be upheld if we are to continue to have this kind of country that was established two hundred years ago. It is the foundation of civilized society.

Can we allow these kinds of things to happen whenever anyone in the Government decides that it should be done because they don't like someone or because they think he is bad or disagree with his belief? And then sit around and drink champagne after it is over? What would this country become? What would happen to our freedoms and our rights?

This isn't patriotism. It is anarchy, the beginnings of a police state.

Who would be safe? Who would be free? Everyone would be afraid to be controversial or to know someone who is controversial.

Is this the kind of country we want? Is this the kind of country we want to turn over to our children?

Dr. Fielding—he could be any one of us, or our office or our home. Remember what he said? How tormented he was by the suspicion that the break-in must have been associated with Mr. Ellsberg, one of his patients.

He must have wondered about the connection between the FBI attempt to interview him and then the break-in. And he must have wondered what this country was coming to.

We fought a revolution, our ancestors did—we are the beneficiaries of it—to establish those rights in the Bill of Rights. They cannot be violated by people who simply deliberately turn their backs and close their eyes to what would otherwise be obvious to them, who must be conscious of the purposes that are involved and are simply attempting to avoid learning the truth.

The Defendants in this case, all of them, placed their self-interest above the Constitutional rights of the rest of us. They were unfaithful to their trust.

The right of the people to be secure in their persons, houses, papers, and effects against unreasonable searches and seizures means only as much as you, the members of the jury, will allow it to mean. What it means is now in your hands. Thank you.

I believed I had said everything that could be said, and as I finished, I looked into the eyes of each juror. From their expressions, I felt certain they would vote to convict.

The closing arguments had taken all day. As court recessed, Judge Gesell announced that two prisoners being held in the courthouse had seized some hostages. Everyone was requested to leave the courthouse promptly.

Judge Gesell's Charge to the Jury

Because of the escaped prisoners, the Federal Courthouse was still closed the next day, so we assembled in the District of Columbia Court of Appeals building for Judge Gesell's charge to the jury.

The judge's charge lasted about an hour and a half. He covered the basic principles, such as the jury's sole responsibility to determine the facts, their charge to do so only from the answers to questions and the documents in evidence before them, the presumption of innocence, and the prosecution's burden of proving guilt beyond a reasonable doubt. In defining reasonable doubt, the judge said:

> It is a doubt based on reason. It is not any doubt whatsoever. It is not a fanciful doubt or a whimsical doubt or a doubt based wholly on conjecture. Proof beyond a reasonable doubt is proof to a moral certainty, and not necessarily proof to a mathematical or scientific certainty. A reasonable doubt is one which is reasonable in view of all the evidence. . . .
>
> If, after impartial comparison and consideration of all of the evidence you can candidly say that you have such a doubt as would cause you to hesitate in matters of importance to yourself, then you have a reasonable doubt, but, if after such impartial comparison and consideration of all of the evidence, and giving due consideration to the presumption of innocence which attaches to the defendant, you can truthfully say that you have an abiding conviction of the defendant's guilt, such as you would not hesitate to act upon in the more weighty and important matters relating to your personal affairs, then you do not have a reasonable doubt.

Judge Gesell told the jury that it was up to them to determine the credibility of the witnesses they had heard. If there was any conflict in the testimony, it was their responsibility to "resolve that conflict and to determine where the truth lies." In this connection, he said: "The testimony of alleged accomplices should be received with caution and scrutinized with care."

He also mentioned the immunity that had been granted to Hunt and Young and explained that this did not protect either of them from prosecution for perjury if they testified falsely. He added: "The testimony of an immunized witness, like that of an accomplice, should be received with caution and scrutinized with care." I wondered how the jury would react to this, particularly as it related to Young.

The judge defined the difference between direct and circumstantial evidence, and then told the jury they could consider evidence of any attempt to suppress or fabricate evidence "as tending to prove a defendant's consciousness of guilt."

Judge Gesell then turned to the legal elements that must be proved to constitute a violation of the Fourth Amendment as charged in the first count of the indictment. He said:

> A search in the Constitutional sense—and that is what we are concerned with here—is an intrusion or an exploration by a governmental agent or agents of an area which one would normally expect to remain private. The word implies a prying or probing into hidden places—a ferreting out of that which is concealed or secret or has been put away. . . .
>
> When a government agent invades an area in which there is such a legitimate expectation of privacy to look through such papers, without permission, that is a search. A physical break-in is not essential. . . .
>
> At the time that the defendants are alleged to have participated in a conspiracy—just as now—the law was clear that an entry by governmental officials or agents acting for them into private property, for the purpose of searching or seizing materials for use by the government, required a search warrant or the permission of an individual having custody of those materials, except under very limited circumstances which as a matter of law the Court finds are not relevant here.
>
> Such a warrantless entry and search would, as a matter of law, necessarily injure the person whose premises were searched in the enjoyment of his rights under the Fourth Amendment to the Constitution of the United States.

As to each defendant's state of mind or intent, he said:

> In determining whether or not each defendant had the requisite intent, you should keep in mind that a mistake of fact may constitute a defense to the conspiracy charge, but a mistake of law is not a defense.

Thus, if one of the defendants honestly believed that a valid warrant had been obtained, such a mistake of fact would render him innocent of the alleged conspiracy because it cannot be said that he intended to conduct a warrantless search.

On the other hand, if the defendant was fully aware of the relevant facts—that the search lacked both warrant and Dr. Fielding's permission, but erroneously believed that the search was still legal, that would constitute a mistake of law and a mistake of law is no excuse.

In other words, an individual cannot escape the criminal law simply because he sincerely but incorrectly believes that his acts are justified in the name of patriotism, or national security, or a need to create an unfavorable press image, or that his superiors had the authority without a warrant to suspend the Constitutional protections of the Fourth Amendment.

This certainly supported what I had said in my closing argument.

The judge then explained the legal elements necessary to prove the existence of a conspiracy. Here he said:

Now what constitutes a conspiracy? A conspiracy is a combination of two or more persons by concerted action to accomplish an unlawful act. So a conspiracy is a kind of partnership in criminal acts in which each member becomes an agent of every other member.

The gist of the offense is a combination or agreement to disobey or disregard the law. The mere similarity of conduct among various persons, and the fact that they may have associated with each other, does not necessarily establish proof of the existence of a conspiracy.

However, the evidence in this case need not show that the members entered into any express or formal agreement, or that they directly or by word spoken or in writing stated between themselves what their common object or purpose was to be or all the details thereof, or the means by which the object or the purpose was to be accomplished.

What the evidence must show, however, beyond a reasonable doubt, in order to establish proof that a conspiracy existed is that two or more persons in some 'way or manner, or through some contrivance or course of action, positively or tacitly came to a mutual understanding to try to accomplish a common and unlawful plan, here to conduct a warrantless governmental search of Dr. Fielding's office without permission. . . .

If individuals agree to accomplish an illegal object it makes no difference whether those individuals have or do not have the same reason for agreeing to the common illegal object.

There is a question that some may have had political motives, and others may have acted for patriotic reasons, others thought the security of the country was at stake and others may have been caught up by the desire to produce the result whatever the means. It makes no difference why any particular person joined the conspiracy so long as the proof shows, beyond a reasonable doubt, that he knowingly participated in the alleged conspiracy and knowingly sought to accomplish its common objective: the warrantless governmental search of Dr. Fielding's office without permission.

Speaking more directly to the defendants' arguments relating to national security, the judge said:

Now, there is one further point which you should remember in considering Count One: you have heard testimony of several high Government officials and it has been suggested that other officials and agencies authorized or participated in the illegal search alleged in 1971 of Dr. Fielding's office.

However, you must have clearly in mind that the proper concern of the President of the United States and others in high office to prevent leaks of national security information would not have justified a warrantless search of Dr. Fielding's office without his permission.

There is no evidence that the President authorized such a search and, as a matter of law, neither he nor any official or any agency such as the FBI or the CIA had the authority to order it.

National security consideration had been mentioned to explain the background for various conversations and contacts between various alleged conspirators and the nature of the responsibilities assigned to the various individuals.

There were many other lawful things that were done to stop leaks. But, the question for you to consider is whether or not any or all of the defendants conspired to engage in the unlawful conduct alleged in the indictment, namely, the warrantless Government search of Dr. Fielding's office without his permission.

Next, the judge explained the legal elements required for proof of the remaining counts in the indictment relating to Ehrlichman's alleged false statement to the FBI and perjury before the grand jury. He was careful to point out that Ehrlichman should not be found guilty if the jury concluded that any of these answers were the result of mistake, inadvertence, or accident.

He concluded by reminding the jury of their obligation to be fair and impartial:

Now, ladies and gentlemen, you are deciding nothing but this case. Your determination of the guilt or the innocence of a defendant must be reached solely on the basis of the evidence adduced at the trial without any feeling or emotion, without any bias or prejudice, without any anger on the one hand and without any sympathy on the other.

Your sole function is to determine, after weighing all the evidence, whether or not the evidence adduced proves the defendant's guilt beyond a reasonable doubt.

If the jury permits any feeling of bias or prejudice or any feeling of sympathy to enter into their determination of the verdict, then the jury is not properly performing its function, and justice is not done.

I have, throughout this trial, instructed you on the matter of publicity. I again say to you that you must decide this case solely on the evidence presented in the court. You must completely disregard any press, television or radio coverage or reports which you may have seen or read at one time—if you did. Such reports are not evidence and you are not to be influenced in any manner whatsoever by any such publicity.

You are all aware that there has been considerable publicity in this case. You must not let this affect you one way or the other. You must put everything you may have read or heard about Watergate out of your mind and you must decide this case on the facts before you.

The Jury is the bulwark of our freedoms. It preserves the integrity of our Constitutional system. If you believe any defendant here is not guilty do not hesitate to say so. If you believe that the government has established that any defendant here is guilty, do not hesitate to say so.

After he had finished charging the jury, Judge Gesell dismissed them, but asked them not to begin their deliberations until he told them to. This was so he could give the attorneys an opportunity to make any objections they had regarding his charge to the jury. Among other things, counsel for Ehrlichman complained that the judge had not adequately explained the theory of Ehrlichman's defense to the jury. Judge Gesell disagreed. He responded: "There is no coherent statement of his defense . . . his defense has been one of guarding and dodging around various issues."

I had the same feeling. It seemed to me that Ehrlichman had faced a very difficult dilemma: he could have admitted that he was fully aware of what was contemplated and relied on a defense of national security, or he could have denied any such knowledge and claimed he had no recollection of any of the surrounding circumstances. In the first alternative, he would surely be convicted and could only hope the Court of Appeals would overrule Judge Gesell's opinion that national security was not a defense. Carrying out the second alternative of not remembering anything would seem too incredible to the jury and would also end in a guilty verdict. As a consequence, it seemed that Ehrlichman tried to use a combination of the two alternatives. I also felt he did not admit to advance knowledge of what was planned because he still wanted to protect the President. If Ehrlichman had admitted this and claimed it had been done in the interest of national security, the President would have had far more difficulty in convincingly claiming that he did not know about the operation until March 1973. Then, the meaning of the approach to Judge Byrne would have been more apparent.

The Jury's Verdict

It was 11:30 when the jurors began their deliberations. After what the judge had said in his charge, I felt even more certain of a guilty verdict. As court was recessed, I said to my colleagues, "They will be back with a verdict by five o'clock." I figured they would not do much more than pick a foreman before lunch.

I walked across town to my apartment, swam in the pool, had lunch, and tried to relax in the sun. Around 4:30, I walked back to the Special Prosecutor's Office, wondering if my prediction about the jury's verdict had been overly optimistic. When I arrived at the office, my secretary excitedly told me the court had called and asked the lawyers to come to court because the jury had reached a verdict.

Despite my previous optimism, my heart was in my mouth. To add to the tension, it was almost impossible to get a cab on K Street at that time of day. I finally managed to get a ride in a cab already occupied.

When I arrived at the courthouse, Ehrlichman and his wife were also getting out of a cab. I was not sure he knew the jury had a verdict, or whether he was simply returning to the courthouse expecting that the jury would be dismissed for the day, or at least for dinner. As we rode up in the elevator together, no one spoke.

The courtroom was completely full—mostly newspaper, radio, and TV reporters. Before bringing in the jury, Judge Gesell announced that he had a note from the foreman of the jury that the jury had a verdict. He warned the spectators against any demonstration after the verdict was announced.

As the jurors filed into the courtroom, they did not look at the defendants. This is generally an indication that they have returned a guilty verdict. I began to relax.

After the jurors had taken their seats, the court clerk asked the foreman how the jury found each defendant on each count. All defendants were found guilty of the conspiracy count to violate Dr. Fielding's civil rights. Ehrlichman was also found guilty of lying to the FBI, and guilty of two of the three charges of perjury before the grand jury. When the foreman stated that Ehrlichman was not guilty on the last count, I thought this would make it very difficult for Ehrlichman to persuade the Court of Appeals that he had not received a fair trial.

My colleagues and I had agreed it would be unseemly for us to make any formal statement after the verdict. The corridor outside the courtroom was filled with reporters, but we managed to avoid most of them by going down a back staircase to a waiting car. As I was leaving the building, one reporter came up and asked if I was elated about the verdict. I replied that I felt only relief that the case was over and satisfaction in having done my job in a professional manner. I added that I found it difficult to feel elated about being involved in a situation that had brought so much unhappiness to others.

A few days later, Judge Gesell advised us that for technical legal reasons he was granting Ehrlichman's motion to dismiss the count involving lying to the FBI.

After the jury's verdict, the *Washington Post* editorialized that the creation of the Plumbers was an abuse of presidential power, and that the creation of the group and the consequences that inevitably flowed from it constituted an impeachable offense.

On July 31, Judge Gesell sentenced Ehrlichman to jail for a term of twenty months to five years. Liddy received a jail sentence of one to three years, to run concurrently with his sentence for the Watergate break-in. Barker and Martinez received suspended sentences and were placed on probation for three years.

Within the time required, each defendant filed a notice of appeal. Now it would be up to the Court of Appeals to decide whether the jury's verdicts would be affirmed or reversed.

William Merrill's campaign photo taken in 1964, when he ran unsuccessfully for Congress as a Democrat from the Detroit area. Photo courtesy of Carol Merrill.

William Merrill delivers a eulogy at a memorial service for his friend Robert Kennedy, following Kennedy's assassination in 1968. Photo courtesy of Carol Merrill.

In the aftermath of a debilitating stroke, Merrill is no longer able to speak but communicates through gestures. He continues to challenge himself and overcome obstacles. Here the right-handed Merrill is learning to paint with his left hand. Photo by Lance Wynn. Copyright 2007 *The Grand Rapids Press*. All Rights Reserved. Used with permission.

Former White House counsel Charles Colson makes a brief appearance before newsmen after testifying for the Los Angeles County grand jury investigating the break-in at the office of Daniel Ellsberg's psychiatrist, June 8, 1973. He declined to say what his testimony concerned. Photo courtesy of AP Images/Wally Fong.

G. Gordon Liddy, one of the seven convicted Watergate conspirators, arrives at the House Armed Services Subcomittee in Washington, D.C., on July 20, 1973, to testify. Merrill convicted Liddy for illegal activities by the White House Plumbers. Photo courtesy of AP Images.

Watergate special prosecutor Archibald Cox hired William Merrill to head the investigation and prosecution of the White House Plumbers. Cox was fired in the Saturday Night Massacre, October 20, 1973, as Nixon tried to thwart the investigation. He was replaced by Leon Jaworski, and the investigation continued. Photo courtesy of AP Images.

Merrill convicted John D. Ehrlichman, one of Nixon's top advisors, for approving the break-in at the office of Daniel Ellsberg's psychiatrist. Outside the courtroom, Ehrlichman shook Merrill's hand and said, "Mr. Merrill I want to congratulate you on a very thorough but fair cross examination." Photo courtesy of AP Images.

President Richard Nixon pounds his fist on the podium as he answers a question during his televised appearance before a panel of questioners made up of members of the National Broadcasters Association in Houston, Texas, March 19, 1974. President Nixon declared that dragging out Watergate would drag down America. Merrill's prosecution of Nixon's men helped bring down the presidency.

Photo courtesy of AP Images.

More than thirty years after his conviction, Charles Colson holds no grudges and is still in communication with William Merrill. Photo by Rex Larsen. Copyright 2007 *The Grand Rapids Press*. All Rights Reserved. Used with permission.

13

Appeals

They lived in their own private world—one in which even the
Constitution and the Bill of Rights did not exist.

—from the trial notes of William H. Merrill

All defendants and the Special Prosecutor filed lengthy briefs, and
on June 18, 1975, the appeals were argued before the United States
Court of Appeals for the District of Columbia. On May 17, 1976, the
Court issued its opinions.

Ehrlichman

In a forty-four-page opinion reported in volume 546 Federal Reporter,
Second Series, page 910, Judge Wilkey affirmed Ehrlichman's convictions
for violating Dr. Fielding's civil rights and the two perjury counts before

the grand jury. Judges Leventhal and Merhige joined in a fourteen-page opinion in which they concurred with Judge Wilkey's opinion.

The Court quickly disposed of Ehrlichman's argument that he had been denied a fair trial because of the pretrial publicity. It said:

> As to the jurors and alternates selected to serve none had expressed an opinion about the defendants' guilt, although one had heard that there had been a break-in by someone and another had heard that Ehrlichman was "involved." Few of the jurors selected had more than a faint awareness of the Fielding-Ellsberg matter, and none expressed any particular interest in Watergate. None were challenged for cause by the defendants. . . .
>
> The law does not require that jurors be totally ignorant of the facts and issues involved in a case. See Irvin, 366 U.S. at 722–23; Liddy, 503 F.2d at 437. The trial court's examination here adequately probed the question of prejudice and enabled the defendants to ascertain—within limits of reasonableness, and necessary adequacy—what the prospective jurors had heard about the case and the extent to which they might have made preliminary determinations about guilt or innocence. That examination did not reveal a deep seated prejudice against defendants that would make the voir dire procedure suspect.

Judge Wilkey then turned to what the Court of Appeals felt were the two main legal arguments raised by Ehrlichman. The first was that the break-in was not a violation of the Fourth Amendment, because it was undertaken pursuant to the President's delegable constitutional prerogative in the field of foreign affairs to authorize such a search. The second argument was that even if the search was illegal, the Special Prosecutor had failed to prove that Ehrlichman acted with the "specific intent" required to violate the civil rights statute.

The specific-intent requirement means simply that court decisions interpreting the civil rights statute required us to prove not only that the defendants intended to search Dr. Fielding's office, but also that in doing so they specifically intended to deprive Dr. Fielding of his right to be free from unreasonable search and seizure under the Fourth Amendment. In their pretrial motions, the defendants had contended that they lacked this specific intent because they believed they were authorized to search the doctor's office. Judge Gesell had ruled that such authorization was factually absent and legally insufficient as a defense to the charges.

The Court of Appeals agreed that a mistaken belief as to the legality of one's act is generally not a defense to the crime charged. It stated that the specific intent necessary to establish the violation charged against these defendants did not require proof that they recognized their actions were unlawful, but would be present if they committed an act that deprived a citizen of a "clearly defined constitutional right." It added that the right to be free from unreasonable searches and seizures was a "clearly protected constitutional right."

In response to Ehrlichman's argument that Dr. Fielding was not entitled to the protection of the Fourth Amendment for national-security reasons, the Court stated:

> The "national security" exception can only be invoked if there has been a specific authorization by the President, or by the Attorney General as his chief legal advisor, for the particular case.
>
> Neither Ehrlichman nor any of his codefendants have alleged that the Attorney General gave his approval to the Fielding operation; and none has attempted to refute former President Nixon's assertion that he had no prior knowledge of the break-in and, therefore, could not and did not authorize the search. Ehrlichman soars into a novel claim of authority. No court has ever in any way indicated, nor has any Presidential administration or Attorney General claimed, that any executive officer acting under an inexplicit Presidential mandate may authorize warrantless searches of foreign agents or collaborators, much less the warrantless search of the offices of an American citizen not himself suspected of collaboration.
>
> Indeed, for Ehrlichman to argue that the President gave his express authorization to a surreptitious entry and search of Dr. Fielding's office would have been patently inconsistent with Ehrlichman's primary defense

at trial. Such authorization would have been transmitted to the "Room 16" unit through Ehrlichman, and he claimed not to have known the unit planned a surreptitious entry and search. The trial judge, however, put the question of Ehrlichman's prior knowledge of the break-in squarely to the jury, and they found him guilty as charged.

Finally, the Court of Appeals disposed of Ehrlichman's arguments that he should have been tried separately and not with the others, that he was deprived of the right to discover certain evidence relating to national security, and that the trial court should have ordered more elaborate interrogatories to the President.

The concurring opinion of Judges Leventhal and Merhige addressed itself to the arguments raised in an *amicus curial* (friend of the court) brief filed by the Department of Justice. Filing the brief itself posed an odd situation. One wondered who represented the Government—the Special Prosecutor or the Department of Justice.

The issues raised in the department's brief were even more curious, and to some extent inconsistent with the position of the Special Prosecutor. In a two-page memo, the Department of Justice contended that a search without a warrant may be made if there is solid reason to believe that foreign espionage is involved and that there is personal authorization by the President or Attorney General. In response, Judge Leventhal wrote:

> It troubles me particularly because the position is asserted by the Department of Justice, the law department of the Executive Branch, and has reverberations. That kind of assertion of an exception to settled doctrine may lead to an assumption by highly placed officials that the settled doctrine is now "eroded."
>
> The very assertion of the exception by the Department of Justice accomplishes some diminution of the sense of privacy of all. . . .
>
> Citizens whose views are in opposition to the Administration's may be pursued on the ground of some relation to foreign intelligence, although that is not in fact the case. Indeed, in this case it was admitted

that Dr. Fielding, whose office was broken into, had no relation whatever to foreign intelligence, and although that was speculated as a possibility as to Dr. Ellsberg, no information linking Dr. Ellsberg to foreign intelligence has yet been disclosed. . . .

The Amicus brief in effect seeks to rewrite history by saying that the Department of Justice has always sanctioned trespasses, and seeks to finesse the distinction between technical trespass for electronic surveillance and the kind of breaking and entering that was for hundreds of years labeled a core violation of fundamental rights.

Liddy

Judge Merhige wrote the opinion of the Court of Appeals denying Liddy's appeal and affirming the jury's verdict. The opinion is reported in volume 542 Federal Reporter, Second Series, page 76. Liddy had argued that constitutional rights to a speedy trial and due process were violated by the adjournment and ultimate dismissal of the burglary charges in California.

He also claimed that he was deprived of his constitutional rights by Judge Gesell's refusal to enforce two subpoenas to a House of Representatives subcommittee to produce transcripts of the testimony of certain individuals who testified in the trial. Judge Merhige rejected these and other subsidiary arguments raised by Liddy.

Barker and Martinez

The Court of Appeals had more difficulty with how to treat Barker and Martinez. In a twenty-five-page opinion by Judge Wilkey in which Judge Merhige concurred, the convictions were reversed. This opinion is reported in volume 546 Federal Reporter, Second Series, page 940.

Judges Wilkey and Merhige concluded that Judge Gesell had improperly prevented Barker and Martinez from their efforts to show the jury the extent of their reliance on what they felt was Hunt's authority to order the covert operation. Although they agreed that a mistaken belief as to the law or ignorance of the law is generally not a defense to the commission of a crime, they felt Judge Gesell was wrong in not allowing a possible exemption to this principle. They felt such an exemption should have been made available to Barker and Martinez by allowing them to show the jury how and why they had relied on what they believed was Hunt's authority.

The Court's conclusion was somewhat similar to a situation where a defendant claims he should not be held guilty because he acted as the result of an honest but mistaken belief in certain significant facts. Courts recognize this as a complete defense to a crime if the defendant's conduct would have been lawful if the facts had been as he had believed. In other words, if Barker and Martinez had honestly believed that a valid search warrant for Dr. Fielding's office had been issued, they could have relied on the defense of mistake of fact. They did not claim they believed such a warrant had been issued, but instead relied on what they claimed was a mistake of fact (their belief that Hunt was a duly authorized government agent) and a mistake of law (their belief that Hunt had the legal basis to conduct a search, either by having "probable cause" or a search warrant). As a consequence, the opinion of the Court of Appeals consists largely in a discussion regarding the very technical distinction between law and fact. This purported distinction is one that not all judges, and certainly not all lawyers, could clearly explain or agree upon.

The result of the Court of Appeals opinion was to order a new trial for Barker and Martinez to give them the opportunity to show the facts justifying their reliance on Hunt's authority, and a legal theory upon which they based their belief that Hunt possessed such authority.

Judge Leventhal wrote a thirty-three-page opinion disagreeing with his colleagues. He was clearly troubled by the Court's exoneration of those who were actively involved in depriving a citizen of his civil and constitutional rights. He said:

> This case calls, I think, for an opening exclamation of puzzlement and wonder. Is this judicial novelty, a bold injection of mistake of law as a

valid defense to criminal liability, really being wrought in a case where defendants are charged with combining to violate civil and constitutional rights? Can this extension be justified where there was a deliberate forcible entry, indeed a burglary, into the office of a doctor who was in no way suspected of any illegality or even impropriety, with the force compounded by subterfuge, dark of night, and the derring-do of "salting" the office with nuggets to create suspicion that the deed was done by addicts looking for narcotics?

Every violation of civil rights depends not only on those who initiate, often unhappily with an official orientation of sorts, but also on those whose active effort is necessary to bring the project to fruition. To the extent appellants are deemed worthy of sympathy that has been provided by the probation. To give them not only sympathy but exoneration and absolution, is to stand the law upside down, in my view, and to sack legal principle instead of relying on the elements of humane administration that are available to buffer any grinding edge of law. That this tolerance of unlawful official action is a defense available for selective undermining of civil rights laws leads me to shake my head both in wonder and despair.

In Judge Leventhal's view of the facts, it was significant that Barker testified that Hunt told him the FBI was tied by Supreme Court decisions and the CIA did not have jurisdiction. Equally important was Martinez's admission that the plan might have been illegal for ordinary citizens. The judge noted that there was absolutely no testimony that anyone thought a search warrant had been issued.

Judge Leventhal pointed out that Barker and Martinez could not have relied on the defense of fact alone:

The fact that defendants do not assert a belief that the President or Attorney General authorized their violation of Dr. Fielding's fundamental right to be free of warrantless forays into his office takes this case outside the mistake of fact defense, for whatever defendants' other beliefs as to the facts, they would not, if true, establish exculpation.

The judge explained the basis for the rejection of mistake of law as a defense to a crime.

> The general principle that rejects the defense of ignorance of the require-
> ments of the criminal law, or of mistake as to those requirements, is not a
> casual or happenstance feature of our legal landscape. It formed a part of
> English and canon law for centuries and all the time with recognition that
> it diverged from an approach of subjective blameworthiness. Its continu-
> ing vitality stems from preserving a community balance, put by Holmes
> as recognition that "justice to the individual is rightly outweighed by the
> larger interests on the other side of the scales." Great minds like Holmes
> and Austin have struggled with the tension between individual injustice
> and society's need and have concluded that recognition of the mistake of
> law defense would encourage ignorance rather than a determination to
> know the law, and would interfere with the enforcement of law, because
> the claim would be so easy to assert and hard to disprove.

Judge Leventhal then stated that this rule should not be changed for
Barker and Martinez:

> Every mature system of justice must cope with the tension between rule
> and discretion. Rules without exception may grind so harsh as to be intol-
> erable, but exceptions and qualifications inflict a cost in administration
> and loss of control. The balance struck by the doctrine with which we are
> now concerned provides for certain rigorously limited exceptions (inap-
> plicable to defendants' claim) but otherwise leaves amelioration of harsh
> results to other parts of the system of justice. In my view, history has
> shaped a rule that works, and we should be slow to tinker. Consequently,
> defendants here must be held to a responsibility to conform their conduct
> to the law's requirements. To hold otherwise would be to ease the path of
> the minority of government officials who choose, without regard to the
> law's requirements, to do things their way, and to provide absolution at
> large for private adventurers recruited by them. . . .

Citizens may take action in such circumstances out of emotions and motives that they deem lofty, but they must take the risk that their trust was misplaced, and that they have no absolution when there was no authority for the request and their response. If they are later to avoid the consequences of criminal responsibility, it must be as a matter of discretion. To make the defense a matter of right would enhance the resources available to individual officials bent on extra-legal government behavior. The purpose of the criminal law is to serve and not to distort the fundamental values of the society.

The Special Prosecutor did not appeal the decision regarding Barker and Martinez. He decided to retry them, and the indictment against them was dismissed.

Ehrlichman filed an appeal with the Supreme Court. However, in October 1976, Ehrlichman voluntarily began serving his sentence at a federal prison in Arizona.

14

A Look Back

No one—not even the President—can break the law in order to enforce it, nor violate the Constitution in order to protect it.

—from the trial notes of William H. Merrill

Time rushes on, and it is part of our common experience that what was important yesterday seems less important in the face of today's new problems. It is also natural to want to forget what was difficult in the past. However, since those who do not remember the past are condemned to relive it, it is essential to preserve some of the lessons of Watergate.

The investigation and trial of the break-in into Dr. Fielding's office had two important results. First, by Colson's plea of guilty to having violated Ellsberg's rights to a fair trial, governmental officials cannot publicly attack controversial figures who have been indicted and are awaiting trial.

The second important result was Krogh's plea of guilty and the conviction of Ehrlichman and Liddy for violating Dr. Fielding's civil rights. As a consequence, governmental officials cannot break into a citizen's office or home on the basis of their own determination of what constitutes national security. The words of the Fourth Amendment—"The right of the people to be secure in their persons, houses, papers and effects against unreasonable searches and seizures shall not be violated"—stand clearly in opposition to such conduct.

During our investigation, there was the frustration of trying to get information from various governmental agencies, and meeting resistance because of their recognition that they had been involved in some wrongful or improper conduct. Their attitude seemed to be that the activity had ended and that we should forget it; if we publicly exposed what had occurred, it would unnecessarily damage the agencies' credibility. On the contrary, I felt that the public exposure of the improper activity would help prevent such conduct in the future. In the long run, it would also make for a far stronger and healthier agency.

Looking back on what occurred, one must come to the sad conclusion that our government's conduct with respect to Ellsberg, with respect to the 1972 election, with respect to many other events, including the firing of Cox and the sending of the FBI to the office of the Special Prosecutor, was inconsistent with certain basic principles of a democracy. It was inconsistent with the principle that no one is above the law, and with the principle of individual liberty being protected by the Constitution. What occurred points up the need for moral leadership, which is vital in a democracy. Those involved in these violations had an insatiable desire for power and placed their selfish interest in staying in office above the fundamental principles of a democracy, above the public morality that is so essential in a free society.

Many in our history have spoken of this problem. Justice Brandeis, in the Olmstead decision in 1928, put it succinctly when he said: "The greatest dangers to liberty lurk in insidious encroachment by men of zeal, well meaning but without understanding."

Brandeis was echoing what Madison said when he addressed the Virginia Convention in 1788: "I believe there are more instances of the abridgement of the freedom of the people by gradual and silent encroachments of those in power than by violent and sudden usurpations."

Some have argued that similar things occurred during other presidential administrations and went unpunished. To some extent this may be true, and Nixon may in part have been the victim of what preceded him. The simple answer is that this does not make what was done during Nixon's administration right. If there was similar conduct under any prior administration, it should be prosecuted. More fundamental to the point, however, is that what occurred under Nixon was dangerously different from what occurred previously. Under him, such activities were carried much further, even to the point of affecting our personal liberties. His subordinates may not have consciously wanted to change our system; however, despite their intentions, we were headed down the road to a police state. How far this frightening development had gone is irrelevant. So is the question of how far it might have progressed if it had not been stopped.

Our nation's experience during this difficult period in our history should have significant meaning for the future. We managed to come through these trying times successfully. But if we conclude from this that we will always weather such problems successfully, we may be lulling ourselves into a false sense of security. We managed to resolve the Watergate problems satisfactorily only because enough people cared about preserving the fundamental principles that were threatened.

We must recognize that our system of government is a very delicate one. Its continued success and survival is not inevitable. Democracy poses unique challenges for each generation, and will continue to exist and grow in the future only if enough people care strongly enough about preserving it.

We Americans are at once the inheritors of certain principles from our forefathers, and the forefathers to coming generations. How we value and cherish these principles that have been handed down to us, and how we turn them over to the coming generations, will affect whether these principles will continue to exist and grow in the future.

So the lessons of Watergate must be kept alive: the lesson that no one is above the law; the lesson that individual rights are protected by the Constitution. Not as issues of partisan politics, for they are far more important than that. They are as important as the establishment of the principles in the founding of our nation—perhaps even more important, because they are events that occurred during our own lives.

If we lose sight of the importance of the principles that were at stake, or of the fact that these principles were seriously threatened, then we may well be a long way down the road to losing the liberties we enjoy because of their existence.

Eternal vigilance is still the price of liberty.

EPILOGUE

Pat Shellenbarger

Staff Writer, *The Grand Rapids Press*

Experience should teach us to be most on our guard to protect liberty when the government's purposes are beneficent. Men born to freedom are naturally alert to repel invasion of their liberty by evil-minded rulers. The greatest dangers to liberty lurk in insidious encroachment by men of zeal, well-meaning but without understanding."

—*Justice Louis Brandeis, dissenting in* Olmstead v. United States,

1928, from the trial notes of William H. Merrill

In a small conference room at the Grand Rapids Home for Veterans, Bill Merrill awaited a visitor. He gets few these days. This one Merrill had not seen in more than thirty years, since the day he convicted him for his Watergate crimes and sent him to prison. Charles Colson, a man once known as Richard Nixon's "evil genius," holds no grudge. In his own book, "Born Again," he recalled the day he met with Merrill and agreed to plead guilty and testify against the others. "Merrill's relentless pursuit and hard tactics had embittered me," he wrote, "but as we talked this day the anger drained away. He was another human being doing a nasty job, but with a capacity to care about those he felled as much as those he was charged with protecting."

Many of the case's key figures—Nixon, Ehrlichman, Haldeman, Cox, Jaworski, Judge Gerhard Gesell, and Judge John Sirica—have died, leaving only a few Watergate warhorses, such as Merrill and Colson. In the years since Watergate, Colson's life has taken a decidedly better turn. After spending seven months in prison, he founded an international ministry called Prison Fellowship, wrote several books, and became a popular speaker. Merrill's life followed a different route. After the Watergate case, he worked for the Justice Department for a while, took jobs with a few law firms, then was hired in 1990 by a Grand Rapids law firm.

Less than two years later, on Palm Sunday 1992, Merrill's wife Carol, his third and the mother of two of his four children, was awakened by him as he lay next to her. It was not unusual for him, when he was immersed in a case, to sit up in the middle of the night and talk—maybe get up and write a few notes—but this time he hit her in the back. She rolled over and looked at him. His eyes were rolled back, and he was convulsing. In the preceding days, he had complained of vision trouble and stumbled when he walked, but he refused to see a doctor. Now it was too late. Months of hospitalization and therapy followed, but the stroke left him unable to speak and largely paralyzed on his right side. Carol brought him home and tried to care for him, but soon put him in a nursing home. At the height of his career, he was charging clients $175 an hour and bringing home $175,000 a year, but he had failed to provide for something as predictable as retirement or as unexpected as a stroke. The law firm paid his salary for six months, but stopped when it became apparent he never would return. His wife sold his life-insurance policies for a fraction of their face value and sold their house. When their money ran out, she moved him into the veterans home, and a few years ago divorced him.

On a recent visit I asked if he is lonely, and he nodded. He paints oil landscapes and portraits with his left hand and rides his three-wheeler up and down the hallways and sometimes out into the streets of Grand Rapids. A license plate on the back says "Kamikaze Bill." A veterans-home staff member greeted him: "Don't go over the speed limit, sweetie." Merrill smiled and responded: "God damn."

Over the years, he and Colson have exchanged a few letters. Recently Colson wrote that he would be in Grand Rapids to give a speech and would like to stop by for a visit. Merrill was delighted. The veterans-home staff members and volunteers arranged a luncheon, and Merrill sat at the conference-room table waiting. Colson and his entourage strode in. "How are you, Bill? Glad to see you," he said. He put his arm around Merrill and kissed him on the cheek. Merrill smiled and responded, "Oh, God."

"I'm glad you sent me to prison," Colson said. "I came to see everybody who was in that prison as my brother. I'm in prison with guys who pushed drugs. All of a sudden I realized I was no better than they were." He presented Merrill a copy of his latest book, *The Good Life*, opened it, and read an account of Nixon raging in the Oval Office because Daniel Ellsberg had a copy of the Pentagon Papers. The President slammed his fist on the desk, unleashed a stream of profanity, and demanded a team be formed to retrieve the documents and plug the leaks: the Plumbers Unit. "I should have had the courage to stand up and tell people what we were doing was wrong," Colson told Merrill, "and I didn't."

He credits Merrill with helping him turn his life around. "He didn't ask any questions I wouldn't ask. This man struck me as very fair-minded, dealing in the facts and the law. He had a job to do, and he was going to do it. A lot of those guys in that office had an agenda. I didn't think Bill did."

"Are you happy here?" Colson asked. Merrill nodded. Colson said a prayer for him, hugged him, and got up to leave. "Because I went to prison, I was able to help people more than I was in politics," he said, then added, "I don't think I'd ever want to do it again. You were used by God to end corruption in government and set an example for others, but, as I look at things today, I wonder if we've learned anything."

Merrill smiled. "Oh, God," he said.

The Wiretap Law

Public Law 95-511, also known as the Foreign Intelligence Surveillance Act (FISA), or, more familiarly, as the wiretap law, was passed in 1978 as a response to Watergate and the perceived abuse of power by a sitting president in the name of national security.

In 1971 the United States was embroiled in an undeclared war in Vietnam. Daniel Ellsberg, with the help of several reporters, leaked a report that gave a rather negative assessment of our progress in Vietnam (commonly known as the Pentagon Papers) to the media. The Nixon Administration, in retaliation, broke into the California office of Ellsberg's psychiatrist, Dr. Lewis Fielding, in an effort to discover information that would discredit Ellsberg.

Both the Fielding and Watergate break-ins flew in the face of rights guaranteed to American citizens through the Constitution and the Bill of Rights. The Fielding break-in violated an individual's right to privacy as well as the right to a fair trial; the Watergate break-in violated the principle of fair elections. William Merrill makes the point in this book that there were *legal* courses of action that could have been pursued if, in fact, the administration felt that a matter of national security was at stake. Instead it used illegal means to gather information, and then used the argument that national security had been breached and would continue to be breached if it were not allowed to pursue this investigation in order to defend its course of action.

Bill Merrill remarks that he felt that he and his fellow attorneys had stopped this particular abuse of power for all time. Judge Breyer echoes that assumption in his foreword. Yet, less than forty years later, after a brutal attack against civilians on September 11, 2001, within the borders of the United States, Congress was asked to pass the Patriot Act (Public Law 107-56), and it did so in October 2001. Congress also voted to renew this act with some revisions in March 2006.

The Patriot Act in many ways undermines the main provisions of FISA. FISA restricted the government's powers of surveillance to foreign enemies or potential enemies; the Patriot Act broadens these powers to include domestic targets. It opens the door to warrantless wiretapping, as well as warrantless search and seizure. The United States government can now examine personal correspondence, listen in on personal phone calls, read e-mail correspondence, check reading material, etc., without presenting reasonable evidence of cause to a judge.

Our government works because we protect the rights of those who dissent from the majority. We are free to read what we like. We take for granted that if we adhere to the laws of the land, those laws will protect our rights. It is this elasticity—the bonding together as a nation of many disparate elements and the system of checks and balances, which not only applies to the judiciary and executive and legislative branches of office, but includes all of us—that is our strength as a country.

We need to think about the issues *Watergate Prosecutor* raises, the most important of which is the protection of the rights guaranteed to us through our Constitution and the Bill of Rights. We need to read both FISA and the Patriot Act as well as other executive, legislative, and judicial decisions that bear on the protection of these rights. And we need to carefully decide if, ironically, we are not ceding the rights that enrage our enemies in order to protect ourselves in the name of national security.

PUBLIC LAW 95-511—OCT. 25, 1978

Public Law 95-511
95th Congress

An Act

To authorize electronic surveillance to obtain foreign intelligence information.

Be it enacted by the Senate and House of Representatives of the United States of America in Congress assembled, That this Act may be cited as the "Foreign Intelligence Surveillance Act of 1978".

TABLE OF CONTENTS

TITLE I—ELECTRONIC SUVEILLANCE WITHIN THE UNITED STATES FOR FOREIGN INTELLIGENCE PURPOSES

TITLE II—CONFORMING AMENDMENTS

TITLE III—EFFECTIVE DATE

TITLE I—ELECTRONIC SURVEILLANCE WITHIN THE UNITED STATES FOR FOREIGN INTELLIGENCE PURPOSES

DEFINITIONS

SEC. 101. As used in this title:

(a) "Foreign power" means—

(1) a foreign government or any component thereof, whether or not recognized by the United States;

(2) a faction of a foreign nation or nations, not substantially composed of United States persons;

(3) an entity that is openly acknowledged by a foreign government or governments to be directed and controlled by such foreign government or governments;

(4) a group engaged in international terrorism or activities in preparation therefore;

(5) a foreign-based political organization, not substantially composed of United States persons; or

(6) an entity that is directed and controlled by a foreign government or governments.

(b) "Agent of foreign power" means—

(1) any person other than a United States person, who—

(A) acts in the United States as an officer or employee of a foreign power, or as a member of a foreign power as defined in subsection (a) (4);

(B) acts for or on behalf of a foreign power which engages in clandestine intelligence activities in the United States contract to the interests of the United States, when the circumstances of such person's presence in the United States indicate that such person may engage in such activities in the United States, or when such person knowingly aids or abets any person in the conduct of such activities or knowingly conspires with any person to engage in such activities; or

(2) any person who—

(A) knowingly engages in clandestine intelligence gathering activities for or on behalf of a foreign power, which activities involve or may involve a violation of the criminal statutes of the United States;

(B) pursuant to the direction of an intelligence service or network of a foreign power, knowingly engages in any other clandestine intelligence activities for or on behalf of such foreign power, which activities involve or are about to involve a violation of the criminal statutes of the United States;

(C) knowingly engages in sabotage or international terrorism, or activities that are in preparation therefore, for or on behalf of a foreign power; or

(D) knowingly aids or abets any person in the conduct of activities described in subparagraph (A), (B), or (C) or knowingly conspires with any person to engage in activities described in subparagraph (A),

(B), or (C).

(c) "International terrorism" means activities that—

(1) involve violent acts or acts dangerous to human life that are a violation of the criminal laws of the United States or of any State, or that would be a criminal violation if committed within the jurisdiction of the United States or any State;

(2) appear to be intended—

(A) to intimidate or coerce a civilian population;

(B) to influence the policy of a government by assassination or kidnapping; and

(3) occur totally outside the United States, or transcend national boundaries in terms of the means by which they are accomplished, the persons they appear intended to coerce or intimidate, or the locale in which their perpetrators operate or seek asylum.

(d) "Sabotage" means activities that involve a violation of chapter 105 of tile 18, United States Code, or that would involve such a violation if committed against the United States.

(e) "Foreign intelligence information" means—

(1) information that relates to, and if concerning a United States person is necessary to, the ability of the United States to protect against—

(A) actual or potential attack or other grave hostile acts of a foreign power or an agent of a foreign power;

(B) sabotage or international terrorism by a foreign power or an agent of a foreign power; or

(C) clandestine intelligence activities by an intelligence service or network of a foreign power or by an agent of a foreign power; or

(2) information with respect to a foreign power or foreign territory that relates to, and if concerning a United States person is necessary to—

(A) the national defense or the security of the United States; or

(B) the conduct of the foreign affairs of the United States.

(f) "Electronic surveillance" means—

(1) the acquisition by an electronic, mechanical, or other surveillance device of the contents of any wire or radio communication sent by or

intended to be received by a particular, known United States person who is in the United States, if the contents are acquired by intentionally targeting that United States person, under circumstances in which a person has a reasonable expectation of privacy and a warrant would be required for law enforcement purposes;

(2) the acquisition by an electronic, mechanical, or other surveillance device of the contents of any wire communication to or from a person in the United States, without the consent of an party thereto, if such acquisition occurs in the United States;

(3) the intentional acquisition by an electric, mechanical, or other surveillance device of the contents of any radio communication, under circumstances in which a person has a reasonable expectation of privacy and a warrant would be required for law enforcement purposes, and if both the sender and all intended recipients are located within the United States; or

(4) the installation or use of an electronic, mechanical, or other surveillance device in the United States for monitoring to acquire information, other than from a wire or radio communication, under circumstances in which a person has a reasonable expectation of privacy and a warrant would be required for law enforcement purposes.

(g) "Attorney General" means the Attorney General of the United States (or Acting Attorney General) or the Deputy Attorney General.

(h) "Minimization procedures", with respect to electronic surveillance, means—

(1) specific procedures, which shall be adopted by the Attorney General, that are reasonably designed in light of the purpose and technique of the particular surveillance, to minimize the acquisition and retention, and prohibit the dissemination, of nonpublicly available information concerning unconsenting United States persons consistent with the need of the United States to obtain, produce, and disseminate foreign intelligence information;

(2) procedures that require that nonpublicly available information, which is not foreign intelligence information, as defined in subsection (e) (1), shall not be disseminated in a manner that identifies any United

States person, without such person's consent, unless such person's identity is necessary to understand foreign intelligence information (3) notwithstanding paragraphs (1) and (2), procedures that allow for the retention and dissemination of information that is evidence of a crime which has been, is being, or is about to be committed and that is to be retained or disseminated for law enforcement purposes; and

(4) notwithstanding paragraphs (1), (2), and (3), with respect to any electronic surveillance approved pursuant to section 102 (a), procedures that require that no contents of any communication to which a United States person is a party shall be disclosed, disseminated, or used for any purpose or retained for longer than twenty-four hours unless a court order under section 105 is obtained or unless the Attorney General determines that the information indicates a threat of death or serious bodily harm to any person.

(i) "United States person" means a citizen of the United States, an alien lawfully admitted for permanent residence (as defined in section 101 (a) (20) of the Immigration and Nationality Act), an unincorporated association a substantial number of members of which are citizens of the United States or aliens lawfully admitted for permanent residence, or a corporation which is incorporated in the United States, but does not included a corporation or an association which is a foreign power, as defined in subsection (a) (1), (2), or (3).

(j) "United States", when used in a geographic sense, means all areas under the territorial sovereignty of the United States and the Trust Territory of the Pacific Islands.

(k) "Aggrieved person" means a person who is the target of an electronic surveillance or any other person whose communications or activities were subject to electronic surveillance.

(l) "Wire communication" means any communication while it is being carried by a wire, cable, or other like connection furnished or operated by any person engaged as a common carrier in providing or operating such facilities for the transmission of interstate or foreign communications.

(m) "Person" means any individual, including any officer or employee of the Federal Government, or any group, entity, association, corporation, or foreign power.

(n) "Contents", when used with respect to a communication, includes any information concerning the identity of the parties to such communication or the existence, substance, purport, or meaning of that communication.

(o) "State" means any State of the United States, the District of Columbia, the Commonwealth of Puerto Rico, the Trust Territory of the Pacific Islands, and any territory or possession of the United States.

AUTHORIZATION FOR ELECTRONIC SURVEILLANCE
FOR FOREIGN INTELLIGENCE PURPOSES

Sec. 102. (a) (1) Notwithstanding any other law, the President, through the Attorney General, may authorize electronic surveillance without a court order under this title to acquire foreign intelligence information for periods of up to one year if the Attorney General certifies in writing under oath that—

(A) the electronic surveillance is solely directed at—

(i) the acquisition of the contents of communications transmitted by means of communications used exclusively between or among foreign powers, as defined in section 101 (a) (1), (2), or (3); or

(ii) the acquisition of technical intelligence, other than the spoken communications of individuals, from property or premises under the open and exclusive control of a foreign power, as defined in section 101 (a) (1), (2), or (3) ;

(B) there is no substantial likelihood that the surveillance will acquire the contents of any communication to which a United States person is a party; and

(C) the proposed minimization procedures with respect to such surveillance meet the definition of minimization procedures under section 101 (h); and

if the Attorney General reports such minimization procedures and any changed thereto to the House Permanent Select Committee on Intelligence and the Senate Select Committee on Intelligence at least thirty days prior to their effective date, unless the Attorney General determines immediate action is required and notifies the committees immediately of such minimization procedures and the reason for their becoming effective immediately.

(2) An electronic surveillance authorized by this subsection may be conducted only in accordance with the Attorney General's certification and the minimization procedures and shall report such assessments to the House Permanent Select Committee on Intelligence and the Senate Select Committee on Intelligence under the provisions of section 108 (a).

(3) The Attorney General shall immediately transmit under seal to the court established under section 103 (a) a copy of his certification. Such certification shall be maintained under security measures established by the Chief Justice with the concurrence of the Attorney General, in consultation with the Director of Central Intelligence, and shall remain sealed unless—

(A) an application for a court order with respect to the surveillance is made under sections 101 (h) (4) and 104; or

(B) the certification is necessary to determine the legality of the surveillance under section 106 (f).

(4) With respect to electronic surveillance authorized by this subsection, the Attorney General may direct a specified communication common carrier to—

(A) furnish all information, facilities, or technical assistance necessary to accomplish the electronic surveillance in such a manner as will protect its secrecy and produce a minimum of interference with the services that such carrier is providing its customers; and

(B) maintain under security procedures approved by the Attorney General and the Director of Central Intelligence any records concerning the surveillance or the aid furnished which such carrier wishes to retain.

The government shall compensate, at the prevailing rate, such carrier for furnishing such aid.

(b) Applications for a court order under this title are authorized if the President has, by written authorization, empowered the Attorney General to approve applications to the court having jurisdiction under section 103, and a judge to whom an application is made may, notwithstanding any other law, grant an order, in conformity with section 105, approving electronic surveillance of a foreign power or an agent of a foreign power for the purpose of obtaining foreign intelligence information, except that the court shall not have jurisdiction to grant any order approving electronic surveillance directed solely as described in paragraph (1) (A) of subsection (a) unless such surveillance may involve the acquisition of communications of any United States person.

DESIGNATION OF JUDGES

SEC. 103 (a) The Chief Justice of the United States shall publicly designate seven district court judges from seven of the United States judicial circuits who shall constitute a court which shall have jurisdiction to hear applications for and grant orders approving electronic surveillance anywhere within the United States under the procedures set forth in this Act, except that no judge designated under this subsection shall hear the same application for electronic surveillance under this Act which has been denied previously by another judge designated under this subsection. If any judge so designated denies an application for an order authorizing electronic surveillance under this Act, such judge shall provide immediately for the record a written statement of each reason for his decision and, on motion of the United States, the record shall be transmitted, under seal, to the court of review established in subsection (b).

(b) The Chief Justice shall publicly designate three judges, one of whom shall be publicly designated as the presiding judge, from the United States district or courts of appeals who together shall comprise a court of review which shall have jurisdiction to review the denial of any application made under this Act. If such court determines that the application was properly denied, the court shall immediately provide for the record a written statement of each reason for its decision and, on petition of the United States for a writ of certiorari, the record shall be transmitted under seal to the Supreme Court, which shall have jurisdiction to review such decision.

(c) Proceedings under this Act shall be conducted as expeditiously as possible. The record of proceedings under this Act, including applications made and orders granted, shall be maintained under security measures established by the Chief Justice in consultation with the Attorney General and the Director of Central Intelligence.

(d) Each judge designated under this section shall so serve for a maximum of seven years and shall not be eligible for redesignation, except that the judges first designated under subsection (a) shall be designated for terms of from one to seven years so that one term expires each year, and that judges first designated under subsection (b) shall be designated for terms of three, five, and seven years.

APPLICATION FOR AN ORDER

SEC. 104 (a) Each application for an order approving electronic surveillance under this title shall be made by a Federal officer in writing upon oath or affirmation to a judge having jurisdiction under section 103. Each application shall require the approval of the Attorney General based upon his finding that it satisfies the criteria and requirements of such application as set forth in this title. It shall include—

(1) the identity of the Federal officer making the application;

(2) the authority conferred on the Attorney General by the President of the United States and the approval of the Attorney General to make the application;

(3) the identity, if known, or a description of the target of the electronic surveillance;

(4) a statement of the facts and circumstances relied upon by the applicant to justify his belief that—

(A) the target of the electronic surveillance is a foreign power or an agent of a foreign power; and

(B) each of the facilities or places at which the electronic surveillance is directed is being used, or is about to be used, by a foreign power or an agent of a foreign power;

(5) a statement of the proposed minimization procedures;

(6) a detailed description of the nature of the information sought and the type of communications or activities to be subjected to the surveillance;

(7) a certification or certifications by the Assistant to the President for National Security Affairs or an executive branch official or officials designated by the President from among those executive officers employed in the area of national security or defense and appointed by the President with the advice and consent of the Senate—

(A) that the certifying official deems the information sought to be foreign intelligence information;

(B) that the purpose of the surveillance is to obtain foreign intelligence information;

(C) that such information cannot reasonably be obtained by normal investigative techniques;

(D) that designates the type of foreign intelligence information being sough according to the categories described in section 101 (e); and

(E) including a statement of the basis for the certification that—

(i) the information sought is the type of foreign intelligence information designated; and

(ii) such information cannot reasonably be obtained by normal investigative techniques;

(8) a statement of the means by which the surveillance will be effected and a statement whether physical entry is required to effect that surveillance;

(9) a statement of the facts concerning all previous applications that have been made to any judge under this title involving any of the persons, facilities, or places specified in the application, and the action taken on each previous applications;

(10) a statement of the period of time for which the electronic surveillance is required to be maintained, and if the nature of the intelligence

gathering is such that the approval of the use of electronic surveillance under this title should not automatically terminate when the described type of information has first been obtained, a description of facts supporting the belief that additional information of the same type will be obtained thereafter; and

(11) whenever more than one electronic, mechanical or other surveillance device is to be used with respect to a particular proposed electronic surveillance, the coverage of the devices involved and what minimization procedures apply to information acquired by each device.

(b) Whenever the target of the electronic surveillance is a foreign power, as defined in section 101 (a) (1), (2), or (3), and each of the facilities or places at which the surveillance is directed is owned, leased, or exclusively used by that foreign power, the application need not contain the information required by paragraphs (6), (7) (E), (8) and (11) of subsection (a), but shall state whether physical entry is required to effect the surveillance and shall contain such information about the surveillance techniques and communications or other information concerning United States persons likely to be obtained as may be necessary to assess the proposed minimization procedures.

(c) The Attorney General may required any other affidavit or certification from any other officer in connection with the application.

(d) The judge may require the applicant to furnish such other information as may be necessary to make the determinations required by section 105.

ISSUANCE OF AN ORDER

SEC. 105. (a) Upon an application made pursuant to section 104, the judge shall enter an ex parte order as requested or as modified approving the electronic surveillance if he finds that—

(1) the President has authorized the Attorney General to approve applications for electronic surveillance for foreign intelligence information;

(2) the application has been made by a Federal officer and approved by the Attorney General;

(3) on the basis of the facts submitted by the applicant there is a probable cause to believe that—

(A) the target of the electronic surveillance is a foreign power or an agent of a foreign power: *Provided*, That no United States person may be considered a foreign power or an agent of foreign power solely on the basis of activities protected by the first amendment to the Constitution of the United States; and

(B) each of the facilities or places at which the electronic surveillance is directed is being used, or is about to be used, by a foreign power or an agent of a foreign power;

(4) the proposed minimization procedures meet the definition of minimization procedures under section 101 (h); and

(5) the application which has been filed contains all statements and certifications required by section 104 and, if the target is a United States person, the certification or certifications are not clearly erroneous on the basis of the statement made under section 104 (a) (7) (E) and any other information furnished under section 104 (d).

(b) An order approving an electronic surveillance under this section shall—

(1) specify—

(A) the identity, if known, or a description of the target of the electronic surveillance;

(B) the nature and location of each of the facilities or places at which the electronic surveillance will be directed;

(c) the type of information sought to be acquired and the type of communications or activities to be subjected to the surveillance;

(D) the means by which the electronic surveillance will be effected and whether physical entry will be used to effect the surveillance;

(E) the period of time during which the electronic surveillance is approved; and

(F) whenever more than one electronic, mechanical, or other

surveillance device is to be used under the order, the authorized coverage of the devices involved and what minimization procedures shall apply to information subject to acquisition be each device; and

(2) direct—

(A) that the minimization procedures be followed;

(B) that upon the request of the applicant, a specified communication or other common carrier, landlord, custodian, or other specified person furnish the applicant forthwith all information, facilities, or technical assistance necessary to accomplish the electronic surveillance in such a manner as will protect its secrecy and produce a minimum of interference with the services that such carrier, landlord, custodian, or other person is providing that target of electronic surveillance;

(C) that such carrier, landlord, custodian, or other person maintain under security procedures approved by the Attorney General and the Director of Central Intelligence any records concerning the surveillance or the aid furnished that such person wishes to retain; and

(D) that the applicant compensate, at the prevailing rate, such carrier, landlord, custodian, or other person for furnishing such aid.

(c) Whenever the target of the electronic surveillance is a foreign power, as defined in section 101 (a) (1), (2), or (3), and each of the facilities or places at which the surveillance is directed or owned, leased, or exclusively used by that foreign power, the order need not contain the information required by subparagraphs (C), (D), and (F) of subsection (b) (1), but shall generally describe the information sought, the communications or activities to be subjected to the surveillance, and the type of electronic surveillance involved, including whether physical entry is required.

(d) (1) An order issued under this section may approve an electronic surveillance for the period necessary to achieve its purpose, or for ninety days, whichever is less, except that an order under this section shall approve an electronic surveillance targeted against a foreign power, as defined in section 101 (a) (1), (2), or (3), for the period specified in the application or for one year, whichever is less.

(2) Extensions of an order issued under this title may be granted on the same basis as an original order upon an application for an extension and new findings made in the same manner as required for an original order, except that an extension of an order under this Act for a surveillance targeted against a foreign power, as defined in section 101 (a) (5) or (6), or against a foreign power as defined in section 101 (a) (4) that is not a United States person, may be for a period not to exceed one year if the judge finds probable cause to believe that no communication of any individual United States person will be acquired during the period.

(3) At or before the end of the period of time for which electronic surveillance is approved by an order or an extension, the judge may assess compliance with the minimization procedures by reviewing the circumstances under which information concerning United States persons was acquired, retained, or disseminated.

(e) Notwithstanding any other provision of this title, when the Attorney General reasonably determines that—

(1) an emergency situation exists with respect to the employment of electronic surveillance to obtain foreign intelligence information before an order authorizing such surveillance can with due diligence be obtained; and

(2) the factual basis for issuance of an order under this title to approve such surveillance exists;

he may authorize the emergency employment of electronic surveillance if a judge having jurisdiction under section 103 is informed by the Attorney General or his designee at the time of such authorization that the decision has been made to employ emergency electronic surveillance and if an application in accordance with this title is made to that judge as soon as practicable, but not more than twenty-four hours after the Attorney General authorizes such surveillance. If the Attorney General authorizes such emergency employment of electronic surveillance, he shall require that the minimization procedures required by this title for the issuance of a judicial order be followed. In the absence of a judicial order approving such electronic surveillance, the surveillance shall terminate when the information sought it obtained, when the application for the order is denied, or after the expiration of twenty-four hours from the time of authorization by the Attorney General, whichever is earliest. In the event that such application for approval is denied, or in any other case where the electronic surveillance is terminated and no order is issues approving the surveillances, no information obtained or evidence derived from such surveillance shall be received in evidence or otherwise disclosed in any trial, hearing, or other proceeding in or before any court, grand jury, department, office, agency, regulatory body, legislative committee, or other authority of the United States, a State, or political subdivision thereof, and no information concerning any United States person acquired from such surveillance shall subsequently be used or disclosed in any other manner by Federal officers or employees without the consent of such person, except with the approval of the Attorney General if the information indicates a threat of death or serious bodily harm to any person. A denial of the application made under this subsection may be reviewed as provided in section 103.

(f) Notwithstanding any other provision of this title, officers, employees, or agents of the United States are authorized in the normal course of their official duties to conduct electronic surveillance not targeted against the communications of any particular person or persons, under procedures approved by the Attorney General, solely to—

(1) test the capability of electronic equipment, if—

(A) it is not reasonable to obtain the consent of the persons incidentally subjected to the surveillance;

(B) the test is limited in extent and duration to that necessary to determine the capability of the equipment;

(C) the contents of any communication acquired are retained and used only for the purpose of determining the capability of the equipment, are disclosed only to test personnel, and are destroyed before or immediately upon completion of the test; and :

(D) *Provided*, That the test may exceed ninety days only with the prior approval of the Attorney General;

(2) determine the existence and capability of electronic surveillance equipment being used by persons not authorized to conduct electronic surveillance, if—

(A) it is not reasonable to obtain the consent of persons incidentally subjected to the surveillance;

(B) such electronic surveillance is limited in extent and duration to that necessary to determine the existence and capability of such equipment; and

(C) any information acquired by such surveillance is used only to enforce chapter 119 of title 18, United States Code, or section 605 of the Communications Act of 1934, or to protect information from unauthorized surveillance; or

(3) train intelligence personnel in the use of electronic surveillance equipment, if—

(A) it is not reasonable to—

(i) obtain the consent of the persons incidentally subjected to the surveillance;

(ii) train persons in the course of surveillances otherwise authorized by this title; or

(iii) train persons in the use of such equipment without engaging in electronic surveillance;

(B) such electronic surveillance is limited in extent and duration to that necessary to train the personnel in the use of the equipment; and

(C) no contents of any communication acquired are retained or disseminated for any purpose, but are destroyed as soon as reasonably possible.

(g) Certifications made by the Attorney General pursuant to section 102 (a) and applications made and orders granted under this title shall be retained for a period of at least ten years from the date of the certification or application.

USE OF INFORMATION

SEC. 106. (a) Information acquired from an electronic surveillance conducted pursuant to this title concerning any United States person may be used and disclosed by Federal officers and employees without the consent of the United States person only in accordance with the minimization procedures required by this title. No otherwise privileged communication obtained in accordance with, or in violation of, the provisions of this title shall lose its privileged character. No information acquired from an electronic surveillance pursuant to this title may be used or disclosed by Federal officers or employees except for lawful purposes.

(b) No information acquired pursuant to this title shall be disclosed for law enforcement purposes unless such disclosure is accompanied by a statement that such information, or any information derived therefrom, may only be used in a criminal proceeding with the advance authorization of the Attorney General.

(c) Whenever the Government intends to enter into evidence or otherwise use or disclose in any trial, hearing, or other proceeding in or before any court, department, officer, agency, regulatory body, or other authority of the United States, against an aggrieved person, any information obtained or derived from an electronic surveillance of that aggrieved person pursuant to the authority of this title, the Government shall, prior to the trial, hearing, or other proceeding or at a reasonable time prior to an effort to so disclose or so use that information or submit it in evidence, notify the aggrieved person and the court or other authority in which the information is to be disclosed or used that the Government intends to so disclose or so use such information.

(d) Whenever any State or political subdivision thereof intends to enter into evidence or otherwise use or disclose in any trial, hearing, or other proceeding in or before any court, department, officer, agency, regulatory body, or other authority of a State or a political subdivision thereof, against an aggrieved person any information obtained or derived from an electronic surveillance of that aggrieved person pursuant to the authority of this title, the State or political subdivision thereof shall notify the aggrieved person, the court or other authority in which the information is to be disclosed or used, and the Attorney General that the State or political subdivision thereof intends to so disclose or so use such information.

(e) Any person against whom evidence is obtained or derived from an electronic surveillance to which he is an aggrieved person is to be, or has been, introduced or otherwise used or disclosed in any trial, hearing, or other proceeding in or before any court, department officer, agency, regulatory body, or other authority of the United States, a State, or a political subdivision thereof, may move to suppress the evidence obtained or derived from such electronic surveillance on the grounds that—

(1) the information was unlawfully acquired; or

(2) the surveillance was not made in conformity with an order of authorization or approval.

Such a motion shall be made before the trial, hearing, or other proceeding unless there was no opportunity to make such a motion or the person was not aware of the grounds of the motion.

(f) Whenever a court of other authority is notified pursuant to subsection (c) or (d), or whenever a motion is made pursuant to subsection (e), or whenever any motion or request is made by an aggrieved person pursuant to any other statute or rule of the United States or any State before any court or other authority of the United States or any State to discover or obtain applications or orders or other materials relating to electronic surveillance or to discover, obtain, or suppress evidence or information obtained or derived from electronic surveillance under this Act, the United States district court or, where the motion is made before another authority, the United State district court in the same district as the authority, shall, notwithstanding any other law, if the Attorney General files an affidavit under oath that disclosure or an adversary hearing would harm the national security of the United States, review in camera and ex parte the application, order, and such other materials relating to the surveillance as may be necessary to determine whether the surveillance of the aggrieved person was lawfully authorized and conducted. In making this determination, the court may disclose to the aggrieved person, under appropriate security procedures and protective orders, portions of the application, order, or other materials relating to the surveillance only where such disclosure is necessary to make an accurate determination of the legality of the surveillance.

(g) If the United States district court pursuant to subsection (f) determines that the surveillance was not lawfully authorized or conducted, it shall, in accordance with the requirements of law, suppress the evidence which was unlawfully obtained or derived from electronic surveillance of the aggrieved person or otherwise grant the motion of the aggrieved person. If the court determines that the surveillance was lawfully authorized and conducted, it shall deny the motion of the aggrieved person except to the extent that due process requires discovery or disclosure.

(h) Orders granting motions or requests under subsection (g), decisions under this section that electronic surveillance was not lawfully authorized or conducted, and orders of the United States district court requiring review or granting disclosure of applications, orders, or other materials relating to a surveillance shall be final orders and binding upon all courts of the United States and the several States except a United States court of appeals and the Supreme Court.

(i) In circumstances involving the unintentional acquisition by an electronic, mechanical, or other surveillance device of the contents of any radio communication, under circumstances in which a person has a reasonable expectation of privacy and a warrant would be required for law enforcement purposes, and if both the sender and all intended recipients are located within the United States, such contents shall be destroyed upon recognition, unless the Attorney General determines that the contents indicate a threat of death or serious bodily harm to any person.

(j) If an emergency employment of electronic surveillance is authorized under section 105 (e) and a subsequent order approving the surveillance is not obtained, the judge shall cause to be served on any United States person named in the application and on such other United States persons subject to electronic surveillance as the judge may determine in his discretion it is in the interest of justice to serve, notice of—

(1) the fact of the application;

(2) the period of the surveillance; and

(3) the fact that during the period information was or was not obtained.

On an ex parte showing of good cause to the judge the serving of the noticed required by this subsection may be postponed or suspended for a period not to exceed ninety days. Thereafter, on a further ex parte showing of good cause, the court shall forego ordering the serving of the noticed required under this subsection.

REPORT OF ELECTRONIC SURVEILLANCE

SEC. 107. In April of each year, the Attorney General shall transmit to the Administrative Office of the United States Court and to Congress a report setting forth with respect to the proceeding calendar year—

(a) the total number of applications made for orders and extensions of orders approving electronic surveillance under this title; and

(b) the total number of such orders and extensions either granted, modified, or denied.

CONGRESSIONAL OVERSIGHT

SEC. 108. (a) On a semiannual basis the Attorney General shall fully inform the House Permanent Select Committee on Intelligence and the Senate Select Committee on Intelligence concerning all electronic surveillance under this title. Nothing in this title shall be deemed to limit the authority and responsibility of the appropriate committees of each House of Congress to obtain such information as they may need to carry out their respective functions and duties.

(b) On or before one year after the effective date of this Act and on the same day each year for four years thereafter, the Permanent Select Committee on

Intelligence and the Senate Select Committee on Intelligence shall report respectively to the House of Representatives and the Senate, concerning the implementation of this Act. Said reports shall include but not be limited to an analysis and recommendation concerning whether this Act should be (1) amended, (2) repealed, or (3) permitted to continue in effect without amendment.

PENALTIES

SEC. 109. (a) OFFENSE.—A person is guilty of an offense if he intentionally—

(1) engages in electronic surveillance under color of law except as authorized by statute; or

(2) discloses or uses information obtained under color of law by electronic surveillance, knowing or having reason to know that the information was obtained through electronic surveillance not authorized by statute.

(b) DEFENSE.—It is a defense to a prosecution under subsection (a) that the defendant was a law enforcement or investigative officer engaged in the course of his official duties and the electronic surveillance was authorized by an conducted pursuant to a search warrant or court order of a court of competent jurisdiction.

(c) PENALTY.—An offense described in this section is punishable by a fine of not more than $10,000 or imprisonment of not more than five years, or both.

(d) JURISDICTION.—There is Federal jurisdiction over an offense under this section if the person committing the offense was an officer or employee of the United States at the time the offense was committed.

CIVIL LIABILITY

Sᴇᴄ. 110. Cɪᴠɪʟ ᴀᴄᴛɪᴏɴ.—An aggrieved person, other than a foreign power or an agent of a foreign power, as defined in section 101 (a) or (b) (1) (ᴀ), respectively, who has been subjected to an electronic surveillance or about whom information obtained by electronic surveillance of such person has been disclosed or used in violation of section 109 shall have a cause of action against any person who committed such violation and shall be entitled to recover—

(a) actual damages, but not less than liquidated damages of $1,000 or $100 per day for each day of violation, whichever is greater;

(b) punitive damages; and

(c) reasonable attorney's fees and other investigation and litigation costs reasonably incurred.

AUTHORIZATION DURING TIME OF WAR

Sᴇᴄ. 111. Notwithstanding any other law, the President, through the Attorney General, may authorize electronic surveillance without a court order under this title to acquire foreign intelligence information for a period not to exceed fifteen calendar days following a declaration of war by the Congress.

TITLE II—CONFORMING AMENDMENTS

AMENDMENTS TO CHAPTER 119 OF TITLE 18, UNITED STATES CODE

Sᴇᴄ. 201. Chapter 119 of title 18, United State Code, is amended as follows:

(a) Section 2511 (2) (a) (ii) is amended to read as follows:

"(ii) Notwithstanding any other law, communication common carriers, their officers, employees, and agents, landlords, custodians, or other persons, are authorized to provide information, facilities, or technical assistance to persons authorized by law to intercept wire or oral communications or to conduct electronic surveillance, as defined in section 101 of the Foreign Intelligence Surveillance Act of 1978, if the common carrier, its officers, employees, or agents, landlord, custodian, or other specified person, has been provided with—

"(A) a court order directing such assistance signed by the authorizing judge, or

"(B) a certification in writing by a person specified in section 2518(7) of this title or the Attorney General of the United States that no warrant or court order is required by law, that all statutory requirements have been met, and that the specified assistance is required,

setting forth the period of time during which the provision of the information, facilities, or technical assistance is authorized and specifying the information, facilities, or technical assistance required. No communication common carrier, officer, employee, or agent thereof, or landlord, custodian, or other specified person shall disclose the existence of any interception or surveillance with respect to which the person has been furnished an order or certification under this subparagraph, except as may otherwise be required by legal process and then only after prior notification to the Attorney General or to the principal prosecuting attorney of a State or any political subdivision of a State, as may be appropriate. Any violation of this subparagraph by communication common carrier or an officer, employee, or agent thereof, shall render the carrier liable for the civil damages provided for in section 2520. No cause of action shall lie in any court against any communication common carrier, its officers, employees, or agents, landlord, custodian, or other specified persons for providing information, facilities, or assistance in accordance with the terms of an order or certification under this subparagraph.".

(b) Section 2511 (2) is amended by adding at the end thereof the following new provisions:

"(e) Notwithstanding any other provision of this title or section 605 or 606 of the Communications Act of 1934, it shall not be unlawful for an officer, employee, or agent of the United States in the normal course of his official duty to conduct electronic surveillance, as defined in section 101 of the Foreign Intelligence Surveillance Act of 1978, as authorized by that Act.

"(f) Nothing contained in this chapter, or section 605 of the Communications Act of 1934, shall be deemed to affect the acquisition by the United States Government of foreign intelligence information from international or foreign communications by a means other than electronic surveillance as defined in section 101 of the Foreign Intelligence Surveillance Act of 1978, and procedures in this chapter and the Foreign Intelligence Surveillance Act of 1978 shall be the exclusive means by which electronic surveillance, as defined in section 101 of such Act, and the interception of domestic wire and oral communications may be conducted.".

(c) Section 2511 (3) is repealed.

(d) Section 2518 (1) is amended by inserting "under this chapter" after "communication".

(e) Section 2518 (4) is amended by inserting "under this chapter" after booth appearances of "wire or oral communication".

(f) Section 2518 (9) is amended by striking out "intercepted" and inserting "intercepted pursuant to this chapter" after "communication".

(g) Section 2518 (10) is amended by striking out "intercepted" and inserting "intercepted pursuant to this chapter" after the first appearance of "communication".

(h) Section 2519 (3) is amended by inserting "pursuant to this chapter" after "wire or oral communication" and after "granted or denied".

TITLE III—EFFECTIVE DATE

EFFECTIVE DATE

SEC. 301. The provisions of this Act and the amendments made hereby shall become effective upon the date of enactment of this Act, except that any electronic surveillance approved by the Attorney General to gather foreign intelligence information shall not be deemed unlawful for failure to follow the procedures of this Act, if that surveillance is terminated or an order approving that surveillance is obtained under title I of this Act within ninety days following the designation of the first judge pursuant to section 103 of this Act.

Approved October 25, 1978.

LEGISLATIVE HISTORY:

HOUSE REPORTS: No. 95-1283, Pt. I accompanying H.R. 7.08 (Comm. on the Judiciary) and (Select Comm. on Intelligence) and No. 95-1720 (Comm. of Conference).

SENATE REPORTS: No. 95-604 and No. 95-604, Pt. II (Comm. on the Judiciary) and No. 95-701 (Select Comm. on Intelligence).

CONGRESSIONAL RECORD, Vol. 124 (1978):

　　Apr. 20, considered and passed Senate.

　　Sept. 6, 7, considered and passed House, amended.

　　Sept. 12, Senate disagreed to House amendments.

　　Oct. 9, Senate agreed to conference report.

　　Oct. 12, House agreed to conference report.

WEEKLY COMPILATION OF PRESIDENTIAL DOCUMENTS, Vol. 14, No. 43:

　　Oct. 25, Presidential statement.

INDEX

58; Kissinger and, 72; Krogh and, 49–50, 56, 74, 100–101, 109, 112, 118–20; law practice retained by, 58; Merrill met, 58; money trail and, 35, 118–19; Nixon and, 21, 65, 80, 95, 109, 120, 132; Pentagon Papers and, 108; perjury by, 74, 121; plea negotiations by, 55, 57, 58; resignation of, 4; Special Investigations Unit of, 12; Watergate cover-up and, 58, 59, 69; as White House staffer, 12, 19, 49, 95, 101; Young and, 66, 100, 101, 120. *See also* Fielding break-in trial

Ellsberg, Daniel, x, 64, 124, 126, 151; attorney of, 100, 102; California courts and, 24, 52, 57, 58, 65, 70, 139; CIA psychological profile of, 18, 20, 23, 35, 64, 108, 114, 121; civil rights of, 12, 30, 39, 64, 86, 139, 145; discredited, xv, 19, 21, 66, 71, 72, 84, 88, 102; Doar and, 72; history affected by, 71; indicted, 12, 19, 65, 88; Merrill's investigation of, 11–13, 24–31, 35, 45, 71; as a national security threat, 18, 72; Nixon White House discredited, xv, 19, 21, 65, 66, 71, 72, 88; psychiatrist of, xv, 4, 11, 12–13, 23, 28, 39; threats to, 83; trial of, 4, 29–30, 64; wiretap on, 18. *See also* Fielding break-in

English Common Law, 33, 62, 77
Ervin Committee, 7, 23, 35, 55
Evans and Novak, 43, 44, 48

Executive Office Building (EOB), 12, 102

F

FBI, xiv, 10, 30, 35, 39, 66, 141, 146; break-ins and, 130; Ehrlichman lied to, 96, 101, 120, 121; Fielding and, 19, 117; Grey at, 3; interviews by, 9; Merrill's fear of, 45; national security and, 39; polygraph expert, 85; and wiretaps, 46

Federal Reporter, 135, 139
Fielding break-in, xv, 4; authorization memo, 16–17, 96, 101, 109; burglars, 100, 114–15, 116–17, 123, 124; California courts and, 24, 52, 57, 58, 65, 70, 139; as a "covert operation," 16, 96, 109, 116, 117; cover-up of, 23, 30, 31, 59, 80, 120; Fielding's description of, 95, 99; as a file search, 116, 123; grand jury, 15, 19, 28, 30, 33, 35, 41, 100, 101; home break-in considered after, 50; Hunt suggested, 100; illegality of, 95; indictment for, 55, 63, 80; Krogh and, 49; Merrill's investigation of, 11–13, 24–31, 35, 45, 71; money for, 16; national security issues and, x, 9, 14–18, 30, 35, 39, 41, 64, 113; Nixon's knowledge of, 113, 137; rationale for, 18, 28, 117; search warrants for, 128–29, 130, 137, 141; Special Investigations Unit and, 15–24; surveillance for, 20, 21, 22,

interviews with, 56–57, 73; national security rationale of, 18, 41, 50, 52, 55, 56, 61; Nixon and, 49; perjury by, 41, 50, 55, 56, 61; prison affected, 73; sentence of, 53, 55, 57, 89; sodium pentathol and, 74; "Straight Arrow" reputation of, 50; trial of, 51–53, 55; trial testimony of, 72–74, 97, 98, 103, 106, 110, 117, 119

L

Laird, Melvin, 110
Leventhal (Judge), 136, 138, 140–43
Lewis, Anthony, 46, 61
Liddy, G. Gordon, xiv, xv; attitude of, 103; attorney for, 98; break-in memo by, 103; Dean on, 30; Fielding break-in and, 12–13, 16, 17, 19–20, 21, 23, 35, 50, 117, 145; Fielding trial and, 98, 122, 134; Fielding trial verdict appeal by, 139; trials of, 79, 96, 98, 115, 116, 139; Watergate sentence of, 98, 134

M

Madison, James, 146
Mardian, Robert, 30, 34
Maroulis, Pete, 98
Martin, Frank, 13
Martinez, Eugenio, 21, 35, 50, 64, 114, 115; break-ins by, 98, 122; trial of, 79, 80, 116, 122, 124–25, 134; trial appeal of, 139–43

McCord, James, 3, 11
McGovern, George, 3
Merhige (Judge), 136, 138, 139
Merrill, William H.: attitude of, xiii, xvi, 37, 149–50; Breyer assisted, xvi, 13, 41, 60, 109; career of, xiv, xv, 5–6, 7, 85; Colson met with, 84, 149–51; Cushman met with, 22–23, 151; Ehrlichman and, 58, 76, 95, 99–107, 108–15; Ellsberg interviewed by, 35, 71; ethics of, 6, 7, 40, 134; family of, 150; on FBI, 45; Fielding break-in investigation by, 11–13, 24–31, 35, 45, 71; as Fielding trial attorney, 69, 70–81, 99–107, 109–13; Fielding trial closing arguments by, 115–26; Fielding trial evidence calendars of, 121; Fielding trial jury and, 92; Fielding trial notes by, xii, 3, 9, 15, 27, 43, 55; Fielding trial notes on the Constitution by, 5, 33, 49, 83, 135, 145; Fielding trial notes on security by, ix, 69, 91; Fielding trial opening statement by, 94–97; Fielding trial strategy of, 70–76, 78–81, 89, 98–99, 109; Fielding trial verdict and, 133–34; health of, xiii, 150; hired by Cox as associate Watergate special prosecutor, xv, 5–7, 8, 9; Jaworski met with, 84; Judge Gesell and, 87; as a Kennedy friend, xiv; later years of, xiii-iv, 149–51; memos to Cox by, 9; national security concerns of, 9, 45; on the national security defense,

123–24; Nixon indictment and, 63;
Nixon intimidated by, 48; offices
of, 8, 10, 45; personal style of, xvi, 6,
7; polygraph used by, 85; role of, in
dismantling Watergate scandal, xvi,
10, 12; unpublished Watergate book
by, xvi; *Washington Post* on, 48; as
Watergate cover-up trial attorney,
69; and White House Plumbers, x,
xi, xv, xvi
Miller, Jack, 5
Mitchell, John, 18, 65; Ervin Committee testimony of, 23, 24; Fielding
break-in and, 31, 137; indicted, 11;
national security issues and, 24,
137; trial of, 63; Vesco trial acquittal
of, 76
Montgomery County Jail, 40

N

Neal, Jim, 11
newspapers, xi; commended by courts,
66; Fielding trial press coverage by,
97, 99, 101, 102, 131–32, 133, 134; on
impeachment, 61; *New York Times*,
xiv, 7, 46, 61, 66; *Washington Post*,
xiv, 66; *Washington Star*, 30, 46,
60; Watergate press coverage, 37,
43–44, 66
New York Times (newspaper), xiv, 66;
anti-Nixon pieces, 46, 61; Pentagon
Papers in, 61; "Subverting America"
editorial, 7

Nixon, Richard: and break-ins, 18, 31,
109, 113, 115; Colson implicated, 88,
89; Colson's Pentagon Papers theft
memo to, 66; cover-ups and, 31,
79, 147; Cox and, v, 43–44, 45, 47;
Cox's staff and, 45–47; credibility
loss by, 73; criticized, 38, 46, 60–61,
79; Dean and, 30, 31; denials by, 78,
120, 137; Ehrlichman and, 21, 65, 80,
95, 109, 120, 132; Ellsberg and, xv, 19,
21, 65, 71–72, 88; evidence against,
130; executive privilege argument
of, 44, 60, 61, 69, 77, 80; Fielding
break-in and, 65, 67, 76, 79, 109, 115,
120, 130, 132–33, 137; as a Fielding
trial witness, 80, 115; grand jury and,
63; Haig and, 61; Hiss and, 19, 65;
immunity for, 63; impeachment of,
v, 37, 71, 79, 134; indictment of, 60,
63, 65; IRS abuses by, 12–13; Jaworski
and, 47–48, 49; Judge Byrne and,
30, 31; Judge Gesell criticized, 79;
Krogh met with, 49, 65; Merrill
intimidated, 37, 45, 47–48; Mitchell
and, 31; national security issues and,
37, 38–39, 76, 77, 113, 124; *New York
Times* on, 61; paranoia of, xiv–xv,
151; Pentagon Papers publication
interference by, xiv, 65, 151; Plumbers'
files and, 55, 60, 61; Plumbers Unit
formed by, xv, 16, 134, 151; power of,
15, 76, 134, 136, 145; power abuse by,
134, 145, 147; presidential races of,

issues and, 39; of the Prosecutor's offices, 46

writs of assistance, 62

Y

Young, David, 12; "covert operation" and, 96; Ehrlichman and, 100–102, 120–21; Ehrlichman on break-in with, 66; on Ellsberg's psychological profile, 72; Fielding break-in and, 16–18, 19, 20, 23, 34, 100; "Hunt/ Liddy Special Project #1" memo, 16–17, 102, 110, 114, 117; immunity for, 16, 17, 127; Kissinger and, 72–73; maligned during trial, 122; Merrill interview of, 100; national security rationale of, 18; sodium pentathol and, 74; trial testimony of, 72–74, 97–98, 100–102, 109–10, 112, 117, 120–21, 127

Z

Ziegler, Ron, xv